THE SEARCH FOR
GOD
AND THE PATH
TO PERSUASION

PETER MAY

malcolm down
PUBLISHING

21 20 19 18 17 16   7 6 5 4 3 2 1

First published 2016 by Malcolm Down Publishing Ltd.
www.malcolmdown.co.uk

British Library Cataloguing in Publication Data
A catalogue record for this book is available from the British Library.

ISBN 978-1-910786-37-6

Cover design by Esther Kotecha
Cover image used under license from Lightstock

Printed in the UK
by Bell and Bain Ltd, Glasgow

DEDICATION

To Heather, our children and our children's children
Deuteronomy 6:4–7

ENDORSEMENTS

A superb, fresh and full-orbed articulation of persuasive evangelism as demonstrated in the New Testament. This book will provide a much needed corrective to outmoded and semi-biblical forms of evangelism, as well as a challenge to enthusiastically engage in reaching Twenty-first Century men and women.

Lindsay Brown, Director of Lausanne Movement, formerly International Director of IFES

Peter May draws on nearly 50 years of reflection on his own experiences of evangelism: one-to-one with friends, to crowds of sceptical students in university missions, and in small group dialogues. The result is this gem of a book that grips heart, mind and imagination from the first page to the last. It should be compulsory reading for all thinking Christians who desire to be interesting, engaging and effective in their witness to Christ. I commend it wholeheartedly.

Reverend Richard M. Cunningham, Director UCCF: The Christian Unions.

This is a marvellous book. It is so fresh, free of jargon and nonsense. I know of no better study on persuasion (Os Guinness being the possible exception with his latest, Fool's Talk). Your applications are so personal and believable, mostly because many of them are from your own experience. Being a physician is a great help, as no one can accuse you of romanticizing the Gospel. You have marvellously woven your personal testimony into the larger biblical narrative. And the use of Scripture is full and rich. Your treatment of Acts 17, 1 Corinthians, the Sophists, Barth, etc., is masterful. Apologies to Spurgeon, but he made a category mistake with his lion metaphor.

William Edgar, Professor of Apologetics at Westminster Theological Seminary and Director of the Gospel and Culture Project.

Peter May has written an easy to read and persuasive case for belief in God and in Christ, arguing from history and logic, without resorting to circular arguments. Peter demonstrates the coherence of the Christian faith and, with illustrations from his own wide experience, demonstrates how this can be explained to others in an engaging way. Using rational arguments he shows the reasonableness of faith. This is not a new approach, though it does contain some fascinating new insights, but is one that the Church has often forgotten. The book should be a must-read for all Christians, and if taken seriously would radically change people's approach to explaining core Christian beliefs. Read it and find out!

Keith Fox, Professor of Biochemistry at the University of Southampton and Associate Director of the Faraday Institute for Science and Religion, Cambridge.

In a culture that seeks to privatise and relativise truth in matters of faith, Peter May makes a robust case for the role of persuasive evangelism. Readable, informative and ... persuasive!

Glynn Harrison, Professor Emeritus of Psychiatry, University of Bristol.

Reason, dialogue, persuade. Dr Peter May gives a thoroughly biblically rooted prescription for those bringing the medicine of the Christian gospel to their circles whether in conversation,

testimony or sermon.
Chris Sugden, Oxford Centre for Religion and Public Life.

I am much impressed by Peter May's excellent book. He has done a sterling job. I have not read a book which combines the Biblical mandate of reason with 'gentleness and respect' so well together. This is essential reading for all Christians.
Bruce Winter is Research Fellow in Ancient History, Macquarie University & former Warden of Tyndale House Centre for Biblical Research, Cambridge.

Peter May's clarion call for reasoned faith and persuasive evangelism is grounded in a lifetime of biblical study and practical experience. Like its author, this book is witty, winsome and wise.'
Peter S. Williams, philosopher and author of C.S. Lewis vs. the New Atheists (Paternoster)

CONTENTS

PREFACE

This is the story of a personal journey, though it has never been a lonely one. I have been accompanied throughout by family and friends. They have both provoked questions and help me find answers. It started at a young age, as life often does! The musings of a small boy deepened into more urgent questions in adolescence, leading to a moment of profound realisation on a Tuesday night in May at the age of twenty. But that sense of 'finding' wasn't an end to the questions. It raised the bigger question of how our secular society can rediscover the truth of historic Christianity. Climb one personal hill and a larger social one emerges beyond it.

These questions include: Does life have a meaning? Does it matter what we do? Is there any real evidence for God? – leading to other questions: Are the New Testament documents authentic? Why and how did Christianity spread so rapidly in the ancient world? And most urgently, why are we failing and how should the gospel be communicated today?

I am grateful to many people who have helped me along the way.

The pretty Italian girl who gazed with me into the night sky when I was twelve, Wilfred 'Q' Burton whose infectious enthusiasm for Christ set me thinking in my teens, the students who pressed me to find answers to searching questions, my medical partners and my patients, who challenged my thinking in so many ways, and the 'experts' in science, philosophy and history who have come alongside and shared their deep knowledge of these 'mysteries'.

A particular debt of gratitude, then, to John Stott and John Chapman, who helped me lay foundations, to William Craig, Gary Habermas and Bruce Winter who have shared their expertise, to Greg Pritchard and Chris Knight who encouraged me to write, to Keith Fox and Peter S. Williams, who have been my colleagues and tutors, and to Stephen Bowen, a close friend for over fifty years and now deeply missed, who despite his terminal illness did the initial edit and greatly encouraged me about the relevance of what I have written. My gratitude also, of course, to my publisher Malcolm Down, who has acted as midwife!

Thanks most of all to 'The Manager', who has shared her life with me for forty-five years – and in a real sense, it has taken that long to write this book! She has been my constant friend and companion, has read the first draft of everything I have written, and still chuckles at some of my jokes. She has also nurtured our wonderful children, who have inspired and helped me more than they know. They, in turn, have so far given us thirteen grandchildren, who fill our retirement days with endless delight. In a special way, this book is written for them, confident in Christ's promise that those who honestly seek God will find him.

I hope you, and they, enjoy this journey.

CHAPTER 1
BEGGING THE QUESTIONS

———•———

Little children ask loads of questions. 'What are you doing?' they ask when I am just sitting in a chair! 'Is that your chair?' and then perplexingly, 'Why?' Many of their questions quickly become unanswerable. I suspect that deep inside they have lots of more complex questions, which they find harder to articulate.

I remember in pre-school years wondering why my father went off to work each day. I got the distinct impression that everything we did was somehow secondary to enabling him to go to London. We saw him off – on time – each morning and had to be ready for bed before he got home.

I didn't know why he went to London or what he did there, but it was clearly terribly important. We seemed to be his 'support team'. Mother would feed him in the morning and again at night. My sister and I were responsible for playing with him at weekends, and for allowing him to practise his story-telling.

Aged four, it was difficult to work out what families were for, but Dad's work clearly provided the *raison d'être*. It came as quite a shock to realise that his job was relatively unimportant. He was a textile selling agent and he did not really enjoy it. He only went to work to support us! We were the 'main act', not the support role as I supposed. It was all very confusing.

A deeper question I recall asking at an early age was, 'Why am I me?' I could somehow cope with the fact that the world was filled with other people, but where did I come from? Why was I here? And why now? The more I gained a sense of history, the stranger that question became. The world seemed to have managed perfectly well without me beforehand. I did not voice these questions a) because I was shy and b) because no one else seemed to be asking them. And anyway, I did not have the verbal skills to discuss the existential meaning of my own self-consciousness! I assumed that everyone else knew why we were here but had somehow forgotten to tell me.

I have often wondered how unusual it was to think these questions at such an early age. Evidently, not very. My wife, who tends not to agonise over the deeper questions, recalls at the age of four, sitting on an outside toilet, wondering why she was not her sister. (Think Rodin!)

From memory and from encounters with my own children and grandchildren, I know that these questions erupt at an early age. Some are difficult to put into words. I remember, as a five-year-old at school, feeling the sense of needing a 'special relationship', a bosom pal, someone to share my life with. I wasn't happy living in isolation, but why did I feel that? Of course, I had parents and a sister, and did not doubt their love for me, even if my sister did lock me in the toy cupboard periodically.

But these questions are both necessary and imponderable. Without a metaphysical framework putting us in a context and giving us a sense of meaning, they cannot be answered. They are among the deepest of existential dilemmas. So George Bernard Shaw observed in the preface to his book, *Black Girl in Search of God,* that if anyone was destined to be damned, it was that person who went through life without ever asking what it all means.

At the age of twelve, I recall a particular episode of reflection. I had been sent off, on one of my father's best-ever schemes, to spend eight weeks of the summer with an Italian family, to help their son speak English. They just happened to be multimillionaires,

with a magnificent home in fabulous Portofino on the Italian Riviera, a prestigious apartment in Turin and a house at the foot of the Matterhorn in the Alps.

I had to tag along with them between these residences and also join them for their summer holiday. We flew from Milan to Barcelona and boarded a large yacht, which they hired to tour the Balearic Islands for two weeks. My mind now wanders off as I recall those magical days! I remember one evening leaning over the side of the yacht in the warm still air, with a pretty Italian girl at least ten years older than me. Together we contemplated 'life'. The clear Mediterranean moonlit sky was reflected in the waters that lapped against the boat. Much of the time we were silent. What an extraordinary world this is. So beautiful. So rewarding. So exciting. But what did it mean? And why does it exist?

She asked me what I wanted to do with my life. How should I know? If only I could get a handle on the project and have a sense of where I fitted in, then perhaps I could work out what I should do.

This was a slow, meandering conversation. Long pauses. Half-finished sentences. More a sense of wonder than the development of a strategic plan. Questions were met by other questions – and an overwhelming feeling of how wonderful and yet how strange life was. Oh, the stuff of memories!

I had no overtly sexual stirrings at that age, but did have a longing for a soul-mate. So I could look at this lovely girl and wonder if I would ever find such a nice, warm, kindly person to spend my life with.

I had no formed Christian belief at this stage, and am not sure that I knew any Christians or had much interest in the subject, but fifty-five years and many questions later, I am quite convinced that no substantial answers can be found to any of these questions outside of a personal faith in Christ. Here is the anchor of the soul, the alpha and omega, the author of the grand scheme of things in which my life now finds its place, that sense of calling, direction, meaning and purpose.

It had been an exciting journey to read in my late teens some of the books of Sartre and Camus, and later on, Nietzsche and

Dostoyevsky. The big questions lay behind everything. Reading the New Testament in the context of the French existentialists helped me to understand the depth of the questions and the profundity of Christian answers. They alone helped me to make sense of myself, my moment in history and how I should live.

As my yearning for a soul-mate developed, I felt I wanted to somehow fuse my life with someone else, and only then would I be satisfied. In my teens I came to see this sense of alienation as a fundamental aspect of the existential dilemma, which was talked about not only by the French existentialists but by the great theologian Augustine 1,500 years before, and the ancient Greeks, a thousand years before him. Augustine said that our hearts are restless until they find their rest in God. This strange desire also resonated for me with Christ's teaching that when a man leaves his parents, he should cling to his wife and the two shall become 'one flesh' (Mark 10:8). Here was the human fusion I craved – itself a foretaste of heaven.

Esther Rantzen, a British television personality, was asked how she coped with life since her husband had died a few years previously. She said she missed him enormously, but had plenty of friends to do things with. What she no longer had was 'someone to do nothing with'. And there is a deep mystery. Over the years, my wife and I have been able to find great contentment together doing nothing! As it says in Genesis 2, it is not good for us to be alone. We are made for relationship.

At the age of twenty, I nailed my colours to the mast and committed my life to Christ. Suddenly, the great mysteries took on a whole new resolution, and from that moment on, I had an overwhelming enthusiasm to tell other people about him. I had made a great discovery! But I quickly found that telling others was not necessarily easy. Most people didn't want to hear about it. It seems that many people do not wrestle with the questions that had troubled me. All too often, they just accept life as a 'given'. But I have also found lots of people who had discovered what I had discovered.

A year or so later, I was introduced to the writings of Francis Schaeffer. His book *Escape from Reason* was quite hard work but *The God Who is There* was riveting. He too longed to tell others about Christ, but learned how to do it by asking questions. He asked people about their basic beliefs, the assumptions they based their lives upon. He found, as I have always found, that people may not like being told things but they are usually quite happy to answer questions and talk about themselves.

Schaeffer described how, when hearing the beliefs of others, he would question those beliefs and gently push them to explore the logical implications of what they were saying. He described their distress on seeing how far from reality their beliefs actually took them. He urged that we should do this gently, for if we suddenly exposed someone to seeing their core beliefs falling apart around them, it could precipitate a major crisis. He called this 'taking the roof off'.[1]

A student at medical school and I lived on the same floor of a residential hall of London University. One evening, I met him in the corridor and invited him to join me for coffee. 'No way!' he said. 'You will only tell me about Christ.'

I had been quite open about being a Christian but this was a sobering lesson. So I promised that I would not tell him anything about God if he agreed to drink my coffee. On these conditions, he pulled up a chair in my room. 'So what shall we talk about?' I asked, and then suggested that we talked about him and his beliefs. It seemed a fair deal.

It was about 10p.m. I asked him where his home was. I

gently enquired about his family background, his schooling and hobbies, his ambitions and values. All the time as he talked I looked for issues that should be pressed a little further. Like salmon fishing, you can stand in a flowing river for a long time before you get a bite.

Eventually, he told me that his father was a communist and he shared his viewpoint. I felt a tug on my fishing line. So I asked him what that meant for him. Eventually, he made the pivotal statement that society was more important than the individual. I pushed gently to explore what this implied regarding euthanasia. I asked him about his attitude to people who were too old and ill to offer anything to society. In fact, they not only had nothing to offer, but they were being a very considerable drain on the state's finances.

'Would it not be better to put them out of their misery?' I asked.

'Yes, I think so!' He agreed, on that basis, that euthanasia should be legalised.

'Of course, it is not just the people who are about to gasp their last who are a problem in this respect. Once they have stopped contributing to society, wouldn't the same apply?'

He was less comfortable about this, but conceded the logic of what I was saying. So I pressed the matter further. Most people past retirement age offer little back to the state. If they are no longer earning their passage, why should society keep giving them money? He sighed. 'Yes, I see what you mean.'

It was time to take the roof off. 'How old is your dad?' Ouch!

It was now well turned midnight. It had taken a long time to reach this point, and I had promised him that I would not tell him anything about Christianity. So we agreed it was time for bed. As he walked out of my room, he said, 'See you in the morning – if

I haven't jumped off the GPO Tower in the meantime.'

Asking questions is fundamental if we are to dig up and unsettle the ground of a person's soul. It requires time, listening, a bit of imagination, gentleness, respect and patience. But I also discovered in my haste to tell people about Christ that it is much more valuable to encourage them to do the talking!

In fact, if you are a Christian and find your responsibility of 'witnessing' to Jesus stressful, try not doing it. Next time you have a good conversation with a non-Christian friend, resolve at the outset that you will not try to speak about Christ at any stage. Instead commit yourself to taking a personal interest in your friend and see what you can find out about them.

I am not a natural extrovert. I retreat into my shell all too easily. I can do the upfront stuff but I also need to retreat behind the scenes. I had been chairing a long and difficult meeting in London and was pleased to settle into my train seat with a book for my journey home. The train was full, and a large boisterous man asked if the seat next to me was taken. I looked at the empty seat and grunted in a semi-positive way. He started to take off his coat, rolling it up to put it in the rack, all the while making relentless, inconsequential chatter.

'Good book?' he asked.

'Yes,' I replied monosyllabically.

As he sat down, he said, 'You remind me of my old university professor!' (Yes, I thought, quite probably – old, bald, glasses, book and probably a raised eyebrow and a despairing expression!) Eventually, I give up on the book, closed it and reluctantly turned towards him.

'What did you study at uni? What are you doing now? Why is that? Were you brought up in UK? What part of Cyprus? Is your background Greek Orthodox or Moslem?'

They were general, open-end questions to see where they led.

After half an hour, he brought the subject back to my book, which was on the fine-tuning of the universe. We soon got on to 'natural theology' and he made most of the running in the conversation. Soon, we were talking about God being evident in creation but making himself known uniquely in Christ. Arriving at his station nearly an hour later, he thanked me warmly for the chat and seemed pleased to accept the little booklet that I gave him, which I 'just happened to have' with me.

Years ago, the Australian evangelist John Chapman gave me some good advice. I asked him if he could recommend a thoughtful tract for giving to people. His reply was classic 'Chappo': 'If you want to use a tract, write it yourself – you will be amazed who you give it to!' So I did. My booklet is called *The Greatest Person?* and is available from the Christian Medical Fellowship in London and can be read online – but I would encourage you to write your own. (There will be more examples of Chappo's wit and wisdom along the way!)

So questions are fundamental to evangelism, and as a medical doctor I became a professional at asking them. We are trained to ask open rather than leading questions, but to do it systematically. Direct questions distort the agenda by introducing your own ideas. So you would not ask, 'Have you got pain in your stomach?' But rather, 'Where does it hurt? When did the pain start? How long have you had it? Is it getting worse? What brings it on? How often does it occur? Does it spread to other places? Is there anything that you do that makes it worse? Can you do anything to relieve it? Does it wake you at night? Is it affected by eating?

What else is going on: Do you get breathless? Are your systems working normally? Are you sleeping well? Are you stressed?' etc. etc. etc.

To engage with the deeper issues of life in a conversational way, we need to develop these skills in talking to people. We need to take an intelligent interest in them if we are to find out what makes them tick. We must look for clues about their spiritual well-being, and give them every opportunity to tell us things and ask us questions. Chappo used to say, 'You cannot talk about the gospel unless you are talking.' That is the *sine qua non* of personal evangelism.

In fact, it is surprising how rarely people do ask questions of others and how readily they talk about themselves. Now we will look at the way Jesus used questions and, in the same way that Socrates did, he responded to questions with further questions.

CHAPTER 2
FOLLOWING SOCRATES

——•——

We have looked at some of the big questions provoked by life itself, and the importance of stirring up these questions in people before trying to engage them with the big answers revealed in the Christian gospel.

Socrates was the great exponent of asking good questions. He taught that 'to let no day pass without discussing goodness and all other subjects...is really the very best thing that a man can do, and that life without this sort of examination is not worth living'.[3]

Politicians talk glibly about society's values as though we all agree and understand them. This is far from the case. Socrates had a famous conversation with a man called Euthyphro. He asked him (and here I paraphrase), 'Does God love what is morally good because it is morally good, or does it become morally good because God loves it?' In other words, are moral values chosen by God from an existing range of values, or do they come into existence as a result of his arbitrary whims?

The former suggests that moral values already exist somewhere on their own and God chooses the ones he prefers. This reminds me of Groucho Marx's famous line: 'These are my principles, and if you don't like them… well, I have others!'

The latter implies that good and bad are not ultimate realities but merely arbitrary values invented by God and imposed upon us in terms of commands. These harsh alternatives have teased great minds down the centuries and appear to pose an irresolvable dilemma. Where do such values come from?

The Christian, however, sees a third possibility. Values do not exist independently of God, but neither does God invent them. The grounding of ultimate values lies in the eternal nature and character of God himself. It is God who is good, just, merciful, faithful, compassionate and kind. As the apostle Peter wrote:

> … do not be conformed to the passions of your former ignorance, but as he who called you is holy, you also be holy in all your conduct, since it is written, 'You shall be holy, for I am holy.' (1 Peter 1:14–16)

Unlike the animals, we understand that we are created in God's image, so these characteristics of God resonate in our consciences and understanding. They are taught in the Scriptures but are demonstrated most fully in the historic person of Christ, who shines as light in our darkness. As the Prologue of John's Gospel expresses it, the Word, who was with God and was God, who was there in the beginning and through whom we are made, was himself made flesh and lived for a while among us, 'full of grace and truth' (John 1:1–18).

It is not therefore surprising that Jesus seemed to adopt a similar approach in getting people to wrestle with the big issues by asking penetrating questions. So in this chapter, we will look to see what we can learn from the way he engaged people in conversation.

The Gospels record that Jesus had a consistent teaching method of using questions. He employed them in a variety of ways, which I find instructive. If we ask why the church is so ineffective in communicating the gospel, it is my belief that we are both lazy and unimaginative in our questioning skills. We can't be bothered to ask and are too lazy to listen. If we do start asking questions, we show little skill in the gentle art of interrogation.

There is another issue worth flagging up here. Many years ago, I was sat next to a prominent Oxford academic at a formal dinner. A Christian friend, who had arranged the seating, said he was pleased that I would have the opportunity to talk to this man about Christ. My friend had great confidence in my abilities but I found it very difficult to engage with this professor and failed miserably. I not only had little in common with him, but he was twenty years my senior. I did not feel I could engage with him socially on equal terms and I knew little about his academic subject. Worse still, he made no effort at all to talk to me!

The moral of that story is that we do best when we engage primarily within our own peer groups – students with students, doctors with doctors, fashion designers with fashion designers. As the apostle Paul put it, Jews to Jews, Gentiles to Gentiles, the weak to the weak. Paul was called to become 'all things to all people' (see 1 Corinthians 9:19–23) and sometimes we also will have to engage with people from a different cultural background to our own. But that is always difficult. Our first calling must be to the people of our own subculture group.

One reason we are bad at asking questions is that Christians each week listen to sermons which may well teach us but rarely, if ever, actively encourage us to ask questions. We need to challenge the view that Christians are pew fodder for the clergy. I will suggest in Chapter 13 how this could be improved.

Now, my Aussie friend, Chappo, helped me to see that the way you answer a question will set up the next question. This must be true in anything that can be called a proper conversation. We respond to what the other person has just said. A person looking to exercise some control over the conversation will be keen to steer it towards some issues and away from others. This can be done clumsily but can also be done with a delicacy of touch.

Some people are very unfocused in their conversations, and ramble from one topic to another, as thoughts pop into their heads. In medical consultations with patients, doctors are keen to head them off from getting embroiled in irrelevant non-medical issues and lead them instead to what they suspect are the nub issues. Doctors do this all the time, steering the consultation with helpful questions.

For instance, with a patient who is complaining of stress at work, the doctor might ask him how well he is sleeping at night. Why would that be relevant? Because if he is waking spontaneously after two hours, it might well be a sign that he is actually depressed, and helping the patient identify and deal with that could be crucial to his recovery.

I listened in on a 'spiritual' conversation recently while on a long journey. The non-Christian was a 38-year-old single lorry driver who was living a long way from home. My Christian friend took an interest in him and asked a range of questions about his upbringing, achievements at school, the things he was good at, his ambitions (or rather his lack of them), his loneliness, where he thought he would be in ten years' time, and what his options were. Casual questions were mixed in with more searching ones. Before the journey had finished, the two exchanged personal details and decided to keep in touch.

Starting from 'cold', this required energy and perseverance. The man opened up personally in a way that I suspect he rarely did. At no time did he try to divert the conversation into trivialities. It was all done in a meaningful but relaxed way, even if it did not get quite as far as discussing the gospel.

So, with good conversation in mind, let us look at the types of questions that Jesus used.

Conversation starters

- Mark 5:9: 'What is your name?' he asked Legion.
- John 1:38: 'What are you seeking?' he asked the two disciples.
- Mark10:51: 'What do you want me to do for you?' he asked the blind man, Bartimaeus.
- John 20:15: '...why are you weeping?' he asked Mary in the garden.

These are fairly standard openings which should not be beyond any of us. It is always a good start to show an interest in people and offer to help them. It would be quite rude not to acknowledge the distress of someone in tears.

His deceptively simple question to the two disciples may have been difficult to answer. Seekers are often unsure what they are looking for. They may be aware of some emptiness in their lives but have difficulty describing it, either in terms of truth, meaning or fulfilment. They are aware that something is missing in life but need help to think it through, as my friend was doing so ably with the lorry driver.

Quite often we walk in on another person's conversation:

Luke 24:17: 'What is this conversation you are holding with each other...?' Jesus asked on the road to Emmaus.

Mark 9:16,33: 'What are you arguing about with them?' he asked his disciples.

It is possible to 'muscle in' on someone else's discussion rudely and inappropriately, but to walk into a lively conversation can be a good start! You can ask them to clarify the main arguments that are being put forward and they may appreciate a fresh insight. You may be able to reset the conversation in a more helpful context: 'Isn't the real issue here…?'

I speak for myself when I say that laziness often stops us from initiating conversations. I am a bit like my car mechanic, who said jokingly to me that he loves tinkering around with broken air-conditioning systems. 'It saves me having to talk to people!' He went on to say that women are generally so much better than men in striking up conversations.

Matthew 24:2: 'You see all these [buildings]?' said Jesus as he left the temple.

We don't need a lot of imagination to comment on something – a building, a news item, a current event, perhaps a picture on a wall – and make constructive conversation. Another of Christ's opening gambits, however, may be more of a challenge.

John 4:7: 'Give me a drink' he asked the Samaritan woman.

OK – there were social conventions involved here! He wasn't expected to chat up a woman and it was certainly not *de rigueur* among Jews to engage in conversation with Samaritans. But the difficulty I want to highlight is our common reluctance to put ourselves in a dependent relationship with others. Christians see their task as trying to help people. We do not readily ask for help for ourselves. Yet by showing our need of others, we establish a context where they can then ask help from us. Going to others for help, whether financial advice, car maintenance or a pint of milk, can provide great opportunities for conversation.

Discussion starters

The next task is to move a polite conversation into an interesting one. Here is one example which might help us:

John 9:35: 'Do you believe in the Son of Man?' asked Jesus.

Of course, he used this puzzling expression to describe himself. It occurs significantly only once in the Old Testament (Daniel 7:13,14). The man he was talking to almost certainly would not know what Jesus was on about. He could not say yes or no! Rather, he asked, 'Who is he, sir, that I may believe in him?' (John 9:36). Being less than obvious in our question may sometimes provoke interest and give us an opportunity to expand on the matter.

Framing a question that has no straightforward answer, that is open-ended and invites a range of responses, can set hares running in all sorts of directions. Here are other attempts by Jesus to open up the discussion:

- Matthew 22:42: 'What do you think about the [Messiah]?' he asked the Pharisees.
- Mark4:13: 'Do you not understand this parable?' he asked the Twelve
- Luke7:44: 'Do you see this [weeping] woman?' he asked Simon the Pharisee.

Rhetorical questions

Many of Christ's questions were rhetorical. He wasn't expecting them to be answered. He made his points in terms of questions that demanded an obvious answer. This was clearly a persuasive teaching device that he used and it features particularly in the Sermon on the Mount. Such questions also hook the wandering mind and help his hearers to pay attention. Let us listen to some of them:

- Matthew 5:13: '… if salt has lost its taste, how shall its saltiness be restored?'
- 5:46: 'If you love those who love you, what reward do you have?'
- 6:25: 'Is not life more than food, and the body more than clothing?'
- 6:27: 'Which of you by being anxious can add a single hour to his span of life?
- 7:3: 'Why do you see the speck that is in your brother's eye but do not notice the log in your own eye?'
- 7:9: 'Which one of you, if his son asks him for bread, will give him a stone?'
- 7:16: 'Are grapes gathered from thornbushes, or figs from thistles?'

Profound questions

Sometimes our questions will hit a raw nerve and become very memorable for that person. I have reached an age when people occasionally say to me, 'I remember many years ago, you asked me such-and-such.' I, of course, have no recollection of it at all and they are probably muddling me with someone else. But someone must have asked them, because it stuck. It unearthed a deep personal truth that came home and stayed with them. In my late teens, Jesus was saying things like that to me. 'For what will it profit a man if he gains the whole world and forfeits his soul?' (Matthew 16:26). That stuck. Here are some others that he asked me as I read the Gospels:

- Luke 16:11: 'If then you have not been faithful in the unrighteous wealth, who will entrust to you the true riches?'
- Luke 17:9: 'Does he thank the servant because he did what

was commanded?'

- Luke 22:27: 'For who is the greater, the one who reclines at table or one who serves? … But I am among you as the one who serves.'
- John 5:44: 'How can you believe, when you receive glory from one another and do not seek the glory that comes from the only God?'

Probing questions

In any sensible conversation about Christianity, we are going to need to do some probing in at least three distinct areas. What does this person already *know*? How much do they *understand*? What do they *feel* about it?

Clearly the relevant knowledge might be about Christ's teaching, or the lack of understanding might be about the biblical worldview. But are they attracted to Christ, and if not, why? A leading humanist once told me in public debate that she thought Jesus was a quite dreadful person because of the way he called the Pharisees 'whitewashed tombs' (Matthew 23:27)! Gut reactions are common. Jesus regularly engaged in probing questions, asking about knowledge, understanding and feelings.

- Matthew 21:42: 'Have you never read in the Scriptures: "The stone that the builders rejected has become the cornerstone"…?'
- Luke 7:41,42: 'A certain money-lender had two debtors. One owed five hundred denarii, and the other fifty. When they could not pay, he cancelled the debt of both. Now which of them will love him more?'
- Matthew 13:51: 'Have you understood all these things?'
- Mark 4:40: 'Why are you so afraid?'

Sometimes we need to be quite firm to press a matter home. John 3 tells us that Nicodemus was a prominent member of the Jewish ruling council. He came secretly to talk to Jesus by night and listened attentively but then asked, 'How can these things be?' To which Jesus replied, 'Are you the teacher of Israel and yet you do not understand these things?' Nicodemus should have known from the Old Testament about the transforming work of God's Spirit that Jesus was talking about.

So we might reasonably ask someone if they have ever read the New Testament or even just one of the Gospels. And if not, why? If they have, we can ask them specific questions as to what they have understood. What struck them most? What did they find most difficult? What do they make of Christ?

We can then more easily ask whether they were impressed by his teaching. Did they find his character compelling? What did they make of his innate sense of authority? Did they find it strange that so much of the story concerns the last week of Christ's life? Why was that?

Clearly, if they are substantially ignorant about Christ, we would then need to probe to see if they are interested to learn about him. Perhaps we could offer to look at a Gospel or attend a course together.

If they are really knowledgeable about Christianity, we may need to ask them what holds them back from becoming a Christian.

Engaging questions

Jesus used many questions to help people engage with what he was saying. Some of them need only minor redrafting for our purposes. For example:

- From Luke 12:51: Do you think Jesus came to bring peace on earth or just cause division?
- Mark 3:33,34: 'Who are my mother and my brothers? ... for whoever does the will of God is my brother and sister and mother.'
- Luke 13:2: '[These people who died so tragically], were [they] worse sinners than all the [others]?'

Sometimes he used a broad, general question followed by a specific, supplementary one, which really put the person on the spot!

- Matthew 16:13: 'Who do people say that the Son of Man is?'
- Matthew 16:15: 'But who do you say I am?'

The parables of Christ often started with a question:

Mark 4:30: 'With what can we compare the kingdom of God...?'

Matthew 18:12: 'What do you think? If a man has a hundred sheep and one of them has gone astray, does he not leave the ninety-nine on the mountains and go in search of the one that went astray?'

Moving the discussion forward

Jesus was also adept at moving the discussion to a more constructive place. Famously, he did this with questions, when confronted by the most slippery mouthed geezers you could ever hope to meet. Just listen to them:

Matthew 22:16–22: '... "Teacher,' [they said,] 'we know that you are true and teach the way of God truthfully, and you do not care about anyone's opinion, for you are not swayed by appearances. Tell us then, what you think. Is it lawful to pay taxes to Caesar or not?" But Jesus, aware of their malice, said, "Why put me to the test, you hypocrites? Show me the coin for the tax." And they brought him a denarius. And Jesus said to them, "Whose likeness and inscription is this?" They said, "Caesar's." Then he said to them, "Therefore render to Caesar the things that are Caesar's, and to God the things that are God's."'

John 6:5: 'Where are we to buy bread, so that these people may eat?' asked Jesus. An innocent enough question, but it led to a long discussion about 'the bread of life' which comes down from heaven and gives eternal life. It continued into the next day and occupies the whole of a chapter!

I think it would be difficult to achieve that in our secular world, but we must look for issues that have eternal significance and be able to bring them into our conversations at appropriate times. And good discussions can last for days!

Provocative questions

John 8:46: 'Which one of you convicts me of sin?' he asked. The Jews responded with an *ad hominem* attack on him. 'Are we not right in saying that you are a Samaritan and have a demon?' (John 8:48). They played the race card and accused him of being not just barking mad, but evil.

Such verbal attacks on the person rather than the issues he is talking about are increasingly common today. We can expect them but must guard ourselves not to respond in kind.

The challenge is to bring the discussion back to objective realities. Humour in this situation can be disarming. On one occasion, Jesus responded to violent hostility with a lovely twist of irony:

John10:31: 'The Jews picked up stones to stone him. Jesus answered them, "I have shown you many good works from the

Father; for which of them are you going to stone me?"'

This worked. It brought the discussion right back to the central issue lying behind his miracles. 'The Jews answered him, "It is not for a good work that we are going to stone you but for blasphemy, because you, being a man, make yourself God" ' (John 10:33).

When I first read that story fifty years ago, such violence seemed difficult to credit. Today, the picture is all too common. Arguments about blasphemy in the Middle East rapidly descend into horrendous violence, while in Britain, violent and abusive *ad hominem* attacks are commonly seen in blogs and emails. As for the question about miracles, they completely failed to see the connection between the miracles and his divine claims. Miracles shouldn't cause a difficulty for any of us, if Jesus was whom he claimed to be. They merely beg the question.

Socratic questions

Socrates was famous for answering one question with another while adopting an air of ignorance. This allowed the questioner to think more deeply about the issue. Occasionally, Jesus adopted this approach as we saw in that enquiry about paying Caesar's tax.

But the most graphic example of a Socratic response is reported in Luke 10:25–37:

'...a lawyer stood up to put him to the test, saying, "Teacher, what shall I do to inherit eternal life?"'

We are not told why it was obvious that this was not a genuine question. Perhaps Jesus had met this man before. Perhaps there were smirks on the faces of his friends. Clearly, Jesus spotted the insincerity and politely returned the question. 'What is written in the Law? How do you read it?' The man was, after all, a lawyer! So the lawyer finished up answering his own question. (Now that is funny, as lawyer jokes often are.) Love God…and love your neighbour, the man says. And Jesus replies, 'You have answered correctly…' And adds, as if to terminate the exchange and move on, 'Do this and you will live.'

The man was clearly wrong-footed. This exchange had not worked out at all as he and his audience had expected. Luke records that he wanted to justify himself. You can almost hear the hesitation in his speech, 'And…er… who is… my neighbour?' This was, of course, the cue for one of the greatest stories of all time – the man who set out from Jerusalem to Jericho and fell among thieves. He was left for dead by the roadside. A priest passed him by on the other side and so did a Levite. These were both religious people, going down the same road from the Temple in Jerusalem. The third man in the story (shock horror) was a Samaritan. He might just as well have been a Nazi. The Jews hated them. Yet this man was the one who stopped, and at great personal risk and expense, he bound up the wounds of the injured man, took him on his donkey to the safety of an inn, paid the landlord and promised to return later to settle further bills.

So Jesus turns the question around. He now asks, not 'who is my neighbour deserving my love', but who behaved like a neighbour: 'Which of these three, do you think, proved to be a neighbour to the man who fell among the robbers?' Can you hear the lawyer choking in his reply? He can't possibly say it was the Samaritan! These people were their enemies. He must have muttered his answer under his breath, 'The one who showed him mercy.' And Jesus told him, 'You go and do likewise.' The hated Samaritan becomes the role model.

Closing questions

A final category of questions must be considered. Many of us have difficulty in bringing a profitable conversation about Christ to a clear resolution. We are outside our comfort zone when being personal and confrontational. What can we learn from Christ about that?

I think the best approach can be seen in Christ's example of starting with an easy question, which in effect is just a point of information. He then asks it personally and presses the matter home:

- Mark 8:27,29: 'Who do people say that I am? … But who do you say that I am?

We might translate that into: 'Who do your friends believe Christ is? What do you think? Are you ready to acknowledge Christ personally as your Lord and Master?'

Hopefully, then, we can learn some lessons from the Master as to how we can engage people in conversations about God. We have seen him talking to men and women, fishermen and scholars, friends and enemies, the powerful and the weak, sick people and outright slimeballs. He constantly initiated discussion with questions. He never browbeats them or traps them in a corner. He is happy to say something pertinent and true, and then allow them to walk away.

Of course, he lived in a rather monochrome culture. Nearly all the people he engaged with were Jews. As such, the Old Testament writings were their background story and their authority. Bible images and ideas featured repeatedly in his conversations. When the church took the gospel to the wider world, they had to engage with all sorts of different cultures; very few of them would have known about the Bible. But some fundamental lessons about engaging with people with questions to create meaningful conversations can be learned from Christ himself.

And they were two-way conversations! He engaged deeply with people – sometimes one to one, sometimes in small groups and occasionally with large crowds. He asked them questions and allowed them to question him.

He was not like some guru who stood aloof, uttering mystical notions. Jesus engaged with real people about real issues in real time. He took an interest in them, asking them questions and responding to their answers.

CHAPTER 3
BIBLICAL EVANGELISM – THEN AND NOW

I became a Christian at the age of twenty, in the run-up to a major 'crusade' in London with the great American evangelist, Billy Graham. I say 'great' advisedly. Billy made an enormous impact on Great Britain, with some twenty missions over a period of thirty-five years from the middle of the last century. His team came in like a whirlwind again and again, and everyone knew about it. The publicity was relentless and it repeatedly hit the TV screens and the front pages of national newspapers. Countless thousands heard him preach, mainly in enormous stadiums, filled to capacity.

So I was in the crowd when he arrived in 1966. With more than a thousand others, we gathered in that great cathedral of Waterloo Station, singing at the tops of our voices, 'To God Be the Glory', as Billy got off the train from Southampton. It was a wonderful reception! The Greater London Crusade was held at the vast exhibition centre at Earl's Court and lasted a month. Nearly a million people attended and some 40,000 came forward for 'counselling'.[4] The final event was held in Wembley Stadium which was filled to capacity with 94,000 people – I was there, though I did not count them myself!

I want to emphasise these statistics at the outset, because while I had some misgivings about the style and flavour of what was going on, no one can gainsay what he achieved. Billy has faced many critics, but for my money, he always had the final, unanswerable put-down. Following D.L. Moody, he would say, 'I prefer the way I do it to the way you don't!'

What, then, were my misgivings? Although I had been a Christian for only six weeks, I had read the New Testament through carefully, three times. What worried me was the atmospheric mismatch. A Billy Graham crusade seemed so contrived and so unlike what happened in the New Testament. 'This' was not 'that'. It wasn't so much the theology that troubled me as the ambiance and the context. There was no slick organisation in the New Testament; events then seemed to just happen.

People at Earls Court made their responses on the basis of the unquestioned assertion, 'the Bible says'. No justification was given as to why the Bible should be believed, apart from the fact that Jesus affirmed the Bible as Scripture and the Scriptures affirmed Jesus as Lord. Christianity was presented as a circular argument from an authoritative book, rather than a linear argument from historical data. It therefore invited a blind 'leap of faith'.

In the New Testament, there were no gathered choirs stirring the emotions as people made their decisions, or long, silent psychological pressures upon them as Billy waited for them to 'get up out of their seats and come forward'. In the New Testament it seemed much more spontaneous. People just became Christians. There was no platform in the New Testament, built six foot above contradiction, to isolate the speaker. Evangelism then happened in the market place, cheek by jowl. So the question I was left with was, 'How should we do evangelism today?'

As a result, I went on various 'how to' evangelism courses – but always came away with the same anxiety. 'This' was not 'that', either! A set of Bible memory verses, valuable as they were, hardly cut the mustard; neither did diagrams that could be drawn on paper napkins, though they could sometimes be useful! Booklets such as the *Four Spiritual Laws* did not bridge the gap and neither did guest services in church, particularly when the guests were invited with everyone else to stand and recite the Apostle's Creed before they had even heard the sermon! There was to my mind something seriously adrift in twentieth-century evangelism, but I couldn't easily put my finger on it. None of *this* seemed to be quite like *that*!

The following year I started at medical school. The student Christian Union (CU) was small but committed. We organised weekly lunch-hour talks and were greatly helped by a number of senior staff, who encouraged us and, when invited, spoke at our meetings.

There was a general surgeon, Miss Muriel Crouch, who taught us anatomy, giving seminars to small groups and lectures to the year groups. The first thing to say about her is that she was a superb teacher. She had taken the trouble to understand the difficulties pre-clinical students had in trying to visualise the internal relationships of the organs in the body. Her lecture on the arrangements of the pelvic floor and her seminar on the workings of the larynx unravelled profound mysteries. But she was also delightful, interested in her students, and always kind and approachable; she was everyone's favourite 'aunt'. And being an exceptional teacher, she was very good at explaining and commending Christian truths. When she spoke at the CU, large numbers of students came to hear her.

One day, in the large common room, where 250 medical students were liable to gather, a girl in my year called Mary asked if we could have a chat. We perched on a sofa and she asked me to explain what Miss Crouch had meant when she talked about Christ's saying that we must be 'born again'. Mary told me that her father's family were Presbyterians, her mother's were Methodists and she had been sent to a Catholic school. Yet no one had ever told her she must be 'born again'!

Clumsily, I started to respond. I had only been a Christian for eighteen months, and had to think carefully what to say. As I did so, another student butted in with a question, and as I dealt with that, someone else joined in. Within a few minutes, several were engaged in our conversation and more joined us. They pulled up chairs or sat on the floor, some engaged vocally, others stood around listening, until some twenty or more people were engaging with me.

I was struggling to deal with so many diverse questions. Conversations went 'every which way' – some scornful, some interested, but everyone thoughtful. As issues were flying around left, right and centre, I had the great realisation that 'this' was 'that'. This is what was going on in Capernaum, in Jerusalem, in Athens and in Rome. This is what I had read about in the marketplace of Corinth and the lecture hall of Ephesus. It was lively, spontaneous, uncontrolled – even a little risky.

After some twenty-five minutes of hubbub, the bell rang, giving us five minutes warning that the afternoon sessions were about to begin. Everyone quickly scooped up their bags and books and headed for the doors, leaving me sitting with Mary.

I turned to her and apologised. 'I am sorry. I was completely distracted. I not only haven't answered your question, I can't even remember what it was!'

She replied quietly, 'That's OK. It doesn't matter.'

'But surely it does?' I insisted.

'No, it doesn't. I wanted to know what it meant to be "born again". It doesn't matter anymore.'

'Why is that?' I asked.

'Well, I just have been. What do I do now?'

I was taken aback and rummaged in my case to find a copy of John Stott's classic book, *Basic Christianity*.

'I suggest you read this.'

To my surprise, the following day Mary returned the book to me. 'I have read that. Now what do I do?'

Mary was a bright student and evidently a fast reader.

'Read John's Gospel,' I said, 'and come to church with me on Sunday to hear John Stott preach.'

Mary eventually married one of my flatmates and they returned to his native Australia, where they have been involved in Christian mission ever since. Whenever they come to Britain, we try to get together. Their eldest daughter and her family are currently missionaries in Indonesia. Nearly fifty years on, Mary is still going strong. Her life was turned around in that brief, chaotic discussion.

She was a large personality – in various ways! She was extrovert and well known in our medical student community. People saw the change in her. As a result of her conversion, a steady trickle of students became Christians. A few months later, I asked another student, a professing atheist, what she thought about Christ. I was expecting an intellectual response, but she suddenly welled up with tears. What she then said is written indelibly on my mind: 'How can I not believe? Five of my closest friends have become Christians. They have found a joy in life they never had before. They have found meaning and purpose in life.'

In fact, so many people had become Christians that I was never able to work out who her closest friends were! Within eighteen months, our CU group had grown from ten to fifty. Recently, the intake of 1967 had a reunion, as one does after forty-six years! (Such parties don't need an excuse – all they need is an organiser.) It was well attended and I could not identify anyone there who had stood as a Christian all those years ago but had given up on Christ since. They still bubbled with enthusiasm and commitment as we caught up with each other's stories.

Looking back, the unbelievers had found it all very difficult to understand. The student newspaper carried many interesting comments. The only way they could understand the change in behaviour of those who had become Christians was that there had to be some kind of CU police force at work. The CU members didn't get drunk. They didn't cheat or swear. The girls didn't flirt and the men were not womanisers. So they developed the idea that student parties were being infiltrated by a secretive CU police, who presumably wrote down names, or whispered warnings in Christian ears. They must also have organised a curfew, as the Christians never seemed to stay out late! They had no other way of understanding the transforming work of the Spirit of Jesus in the lives of those who had been 'born again'.

So, what did this teach me about evangelism? Well, I am sure that humanly speaking, the gospel ran through our pre-clinical students because we were a tight-knit community. When someone became a Christian, it was noticed by others, and as we studied the Bible together, we were able to encourage one another in living out our Christian discipleship.

But as with that discussion in the Common Room, sharing the gospel was spontaneous and infectious. Questions were openly discussed. Yes, helpful talks were given and good books – especially those written by Michael Green – were distributed and read. But the gospel spread largely from person to person, in an informal way. Conversations were happening everywhere, not least at the dissecting tables around dead bodies!

It took me some time to identify what I now see as the pivotal issue. If you look at the 'action' words in the New Testament, that is, the verbs describing what the apostles were doing, English translations are rather misleading. Again and again, the apostle Paul is described as 'reasoning' with people. This sounds somewhat dry, academic and intellectual. Not knowing any Greek, I had no idea what the Greek verb translated as 'to reason' actually implied. Most English versions use this same word. So Paul 'reasoned' with the Jews at Thessalonica (Acts 17:2), with both Jews and Gentiles in Athens (Acts 17:17), with Jews and Greeks in Corinth (Acts 18:4), with Jews in Ephesus (Acts 18:19; 19:8), and was reasoning daily with 'all the residents of Asia' in the school of Tyrannus for two years (Acts 19:9,10)! There are many other words that are used – he preached, admonished, testified, persuaded, declared, discussed and convinced – but the word 'reasoned' is used most often and is particularly interesting.

The Greek verb is *dialegomai*. It means *to converse, to negotiate, to discuss, to dispute*[5] and it is the root of our word 'dialogue'. It implies words going 'across' (*dia*) between two people. It is used, for instance, to describe the disciples arguing among themselves as to who was the greatest (Mark 9:34). We can imagine Paul's lively exchanges in the synagogues and in the marketplaces 'everyday with those who happened to be there' (Acts 17:17).

Consider Paul in Thessalonica. Acts 17 tells us that he adopted his normal strategy (v.2) and this is what he did. He headed initially for the synagogue where he 'reasoned' with the Jews from the Scriptures (v.2). Given what we now know about the meaning of this word, this sounds much more like a discussion in a group Bible study than the formal exposition of a text from a preacher. This was dialogue, not monologue.

Luke now uses other verbs, which draw out the full flavour of what was going on there. We are told he was 'explaining' his message (v. 3). This also implies a two-way dialogue, because you can only know if you are adequately explaining something when you get feedback. It is in understanding what they have grasped so far, and also what they have failed to grasp, that explanation comes into its own.

This is now coupled with 'proving' or 'giving evidence' (v.3). This can only be achieved if one hears the doubting and scepticism that needs to be addressed. You cannot substantiate the truth of something if you have not first listened to the uncertainties about it. You then marshal your arguments to address specific questions.

It is therefore in this two-way process of dialogue that Paul identifies and addresses these three crucial areas – ignorance, misunderstanding and doubt. And Paul himself describes this activity of dialogue as 'proclaiming' Christ (v.3).

As if the picture is still not clear, Luke now says that as a consequence of

1) gaining information, 2) hearing explanations and 3) receiving evidences, that a great many were 'persuaded' (v.4). Here, Luke puts his finger on the missing word in contemporary evangelism, which we shall explore next.

CHAPTER 4
THE NATURE OF PERSUASION

———•———

Imagine a door-to-door salesman calls on your house. You chat for a while and eventually you get out your wallet and purchase his product. What are the processes that have taken place in that time?

When you open the door, you make an immediate preliminary assessment. If this guy looks like a rogue, if his speech is incoherent, if he is shabbily dressed, if – and, according to your personal sensibilities – he has a problem with facial hair, he probably won't even complete his opening gambit. 'No thank you, not today!' and, albeit with a friendly smile, you close the door on him.

But what if that initial inspection is more interesting? The man looks pleasant, is well turned out, has a nice smile, presents identification papers and speaks clearly and courteously. You are more inclined to hear what he has to say. After his introduction, you may well want some clarity about either the product or the possible use you might have for it. So you ask some questions:

'How big is this thing? How far does it reach? What does it cost? How long will it last?'

He has some good answers to your questions and you begin to wonder whether this is something you might actually want. So your conversation moves on to some technical matters: 'How powerful is it? Has it been thoroughly tested? Is there someone in this street who has bought one, whom I could talk to?'

You might then ask him if he has any literature you could study, and if so, could he come back in a couple of days, when you have had time to think about it? He gives you some leaflets and an internet address to browse, and he promises to return on Thursday.

Come Thursday, you have a list of three things you want to ask him. He answers your questions with confidence and produces evidence for what he is saying. You are impressed and satisfied that this is a good product and the more you have thought about it, the more you realise how useful it could be. You happily part with the money and take possession of the product.

When he has gone, you plug it in and discover one of two things. Either it works like a dream or it blows up with a bang, plunging the house in smoke and darkness. Later, when the fog has cleared and you have fixed the fuse, you realise that your silver spoons are missing. 'How did he do that?' you wonder as you telephone the police.

Two conclusions come from this. Firstly, persuasion is a process, leading up to a tipping point, the moment of decision when you open your wallet. Secondly, persuasion is never an arrival at complete confidence. You might be wrong, but the balance of doubt has shifted. You think this is all right, but as we say at home regarding my wife's cooking, the proof of the pudding will be ultimately in the eating. You may have made a mistake!

In terms of proof, we are not talking about mathematical proof here. Outside of mathematics, all so-called 'proofs' are provisional and must be held tentatively. This applies to all the evidence of our senses and to all the findings of science, which is why so many scientific 'facts' get overturned in the course of history, when new discoveries are made. Similarly, I was persuaded when I got married that Heather would make me a good wife. Well, so far so good, but we have only been married forty-four years. She might yet murder me! (In fact, there have been moments when she has intimated as much!)

Previously, we looked at Luke's description of Paul at Thessalonica (Acts 17:2-4). He went into the synagogue and gave them some information from the Scriptures. He may well have been responding to something the rabbi had said, because Luke implies that he engaged in dialogue. This was the format that enabled him to draw certain truths to their attention and go on to explain their significance, as well as backing up what he was saying with evidence. In this synagogue context, this was probably with reference to Old Testament prophecies about the coming Messiah, which supported what he was saying.

Now, the people took time to digest all this and we are told he went back to continue the discussion over three weeks (v.2). We are not told whether he met any of them midweek, but we must assume he did. He wasn't a man to sit at home quietly!

Thessalonica was a thriving and largely Gentile city on a major thoroughfare between Italy and the East. While Paul's normal strategy was to start in the synagogue, where both Jews and God-fearing Gentiles gathered to worship, as in Athens and Ephesus, he readily moved on to the marketplace (Acts 17:17; 19:8,9). In Thessalonica, he was attacked in the market by a mob, which we are told set the whole city in uproar. Unable to find Paul and his comrades, they dragged Jason before the authorities (called 'politarchs') claiming 'These men who have turned the world upside down have come here also, and Jason has received them, and they are all acting against the decrees of Caesar, saying that there is another king, Jesus' (see Acts 17:5–9).

Heady stuff! Paul's reputation went before him and his visit had now become the talk of the town. This helps us to understand how it came about that so many people were 'persuaded' by him. They included some Jews, 'a great many of the devout Greeks and not a few of the leading women' (v.4). His message made a massive impact.

(Luke described the ruling authorities correctly as 'politarchs' using a Macedonian term now confirmed by archaeological findings, and according to the elegant Authorised Version, he described the mob as 'lewd fellows of the baser sort'– and I think we have all met them!)

How did Paul gain such a hearing? If we think again about our door-to-door salesman, and the first impression we gained of him, which determined whether we would listen to him or not, both Paul's manner and his speech must have been attractive. He must have rehearsed his opening lines, having had the door closed on him on previous occasions. He evidently found a way of succinctly expressing himself, which held the attention of his audience. We can get some measure of his effectiveness from the response of the Athenians. They were very keen to hear him out (Acts 17:19,20).

Rhetoric

My dictionary gives two distinct definitions of rhetoric – one good, one bad:

1) the art of speaking or writing effectively

2) artificial, inflated or exaggerated language

We will consider the second sort in Chapter 7, but let us reflect on the good sort for now. It is perfectly possible to use words poorly and ineffectively, and those of us in the communications business need to develop our communication skills.

There has been recent discussion in the British press about two men who were famous for their rhetoric, Winston Churchill and Martin Luther King. Churchill originally gave his famous 'We shall fight them on the beaches' speech in the House of Commons. It was apparently electrifying and members were so excited that they insisted he delivered it to the nation on the radio the following day. He was very reluctant to do this, and in the event, he merely read his original script. This came across as flat and uninspiring – though he used exactly the same words.

Now, this is very interesting. Imagine saying in a loud voice, 'The house is on fire – get out as fast as you can.' Imagine saying it in a way that will induce immediate action, if not panic. Now imagine saying the same words in a deadpan way that no one would take seriously. The difference here is not in the words but the way you deliver them.

In Martin Luther King's famous speech, he repeats the phrases 'I have a dream' and 'Let freedom ring' eight and ten times. Because of the energy and passion he famously put into it, it is difficult to imagine that speech being delivered in a tedious way, but it was certainly repetitive, and could potentially have been a real turn-off.

The art of rhetoric is more than formulating the sequence of words. It is also in the way they are delivered – and that goes for all speech. We can be boring, passionate, humorous, sardonic or sincere – just in the way we deliver our words.

Certainly, the apostle Paul showed rhetorical skills in his writing, as 1 Corinthians 13 demonstrates so clearly, but he evidently had skills in rhetorical speech as well.

So if the salesman on the doorstep is going to sell his product, he needs to give attention to his appearance, his engaging manner, his sales pitch, his descriptive powers, and the clarity of his explanations as well as the force and integrity of his arguments, if he is going to persuade people to purchase his product.

Philosopher Peter S. Williams says that Aristotle taught that rhetoric had to do with three aspects of communication: ethos, pathos and logos; that is, the character and credibility of the speaker (*ethos*), the disposition and responsiveness of the audience (*pathos*), and the content and construction of the speech itself (*logos*).[6] He quotes the apostle Paul who urged the Colossian church to pray, not only that he would find 'an open door' to speak about Christ (*pathos*) but also that he would speak clearly 'which is how I ought to speak' (*logos*). In turn, Paul advised the Colossians in their evangelism to be wise, and to let their speech be gracious, 'seasoned with salt, so that you may know how you ought to answer each person'(*ethos*) (Colossians 4:3–6). So the challenge that faces us is identical to the challenge which faced the early Christians. 'Good rhetoric,' Williams concludes, 'is crucial for persuasive evangelism.'

The same applies, of course, to writing. It is my experience that whatever we write can be improved. If we are writing something important, we must not settle for the first draft. I have just checked a manuscript for a friend, which has already been checked by several people. I found a further thirty-eight errors. He is most grateful! But I was just checking for typos. I left him to worry about the words.

Years ago I read a very helpful little book called *Words on Target*. The title itself alerted me to the fact that words are the weapons of truth. They can be fast, sharp and penetrating, making a deep impact. Or they can equally well be sluggish, blunt and ineffective, going off with a 'phut'. It taught me the value of well-deployed short sentences to arrest attention; the use of unexpected adjectives to stir the imagination; to avoid repetitions; to use dictionaries and a thesaurus to select fresh words; and to understand the difference between strong words and weak ones. The author wrote, 'Economy, energy and subtlety, then, pry open twentieth century ...minds.'[7]

In my view, and probably yours, every sentence that I write could be improved! The stuff we churn out reflects the amount of effort we have put in. Obviously, we should get other people to check our work. But we should be our own most critical analyst. To my mind, the golden rules include:

1) Always sleep on a text and review it next morning.
2) Reread it at different times of the day and in different 'moods'.
3) Read it imagining you were quite ignorant about the subject matter.
4) Alter every sentence that needs to be read twice – if you doubt it, change it!
5) Be constantly asking, 'Is there a better way to say that?'
6) When you think it is finished, then start to polish it. Those final tweaks can smooth out the remaining glitches and make the prose flow smoothly.
7) Never write a book – it takes too long!

Explanations

Billy Wilder, the film producer of *Sunset Boulevard* and *Some Like It Hot*, said, 'I have a vast and terrible desire never to bore an audience.' The quickest way to bore an audience, apart from being dull, is to make sure they lose the plot. If we are to persuade people that Christianity is true, we must make sure that we are making sense to people and that they can follow what we are saying. The moment we use terms they do not understand or try to explain concepts which we haven't properly grasped ourselves, they will quickly glaze over – losing not only the plot but probably the will to live!

It has been well said that 'it is not what we say that matters, but what they hear'. So what words should we use to explain incarnation, sin, justification, redemption, faith and repentance? We have to work at these things. We need sparkling illustrations to carry these ideas. For instance, I like to explain the incarnation as Jesus being the 'human face of God' and sin as 'self-worship'. I describe redemption in terms of buying and restoring a damaged antique. And I always explain faith in terms of trust.

Metaphors have their limitations and weaknesses, but good ones can go a long way in getting across complex ideas. Like parables, they convey packages of truth – and we need lots of them.

However, we should not allow ourselves to believe that Christianity is too complex to explain. It would never have taken off so dramatically if it was. Our problem may be that we spend too much time listening to amateur theologians and not enough time listening to the straightforward questions of unbelievers.

Evidences

Once the door-to-door salesman has explained what he has to offer, there are three basic questions that we need to ask. 1) Is it true what he is saying? 2) What are the implications of buying it? 3) Do I actually need it? Most other questions we might ask come into those categories (Is there a guarantee? Does it smell? Have I already got a good alternative?)

I have often heard people say that the questions people ask about Christianity today are different from the questions they asked a generation ago. Certainly our cultures evolve and do so with increasing speed. So the questions relating to culture will change. But once the gospel is 'on the table' it invokes the same sort of questions that it always has done, because they are not questions about our culture but questions about a very specific and, at first sight, highly improbable proposition that God has revealed himself in Christ. In three broad categories, these eight questions are highly predictable.

Is it true, and how can we know it is true?
    1) Are the New Testament documents historically reliable?
    2) Is Christ unique among the world's religious figures?
    3) Has science disproved God?
    4) Isn't religion just psychological?

What are the implications of it being true?
    5) What are the natures of faith and repentance?
    6) What will happen to unbelievers and those who never hear about Christ?
    7) Why would a good God allow suffering and evil?

Do I need it?
    8) Aren't I good enough for God as I am?

Those basic questions are thrown up by the very nature of

the gospel, and are asked, sometimes in identical words, by both educated and uneducated people in every continent and every culture.

I once sat an exam where (without cheating, I might add) the class had managed to work out in advance what the questions would be. The exam paper was exactly what we expected – and everyone in the class scored the top grade. Well, they would have been idiots not to! If you know the questions in advance, you can get to work on preparing good answers.

Persuasive evangelism?

Now, I believe that persuasion is the missing ingredient in Christian mission. An important Anglican report called 'The Measure of Mission' shaped Anglican thinking for a generation. In its 'Theological Reflections', it set out the 'Ten Marks of Mission', but persuasion was not one of them. It then listed 'Twelve Words Used in the Mission Debate' – but persuasion was not there either.[8]

Yet Luke in Acts records that a great multitude of people were 'persuaded' in Thessalonica (17:4). In Berea, the Jews were 'examining the Scriptures daily to see if these things were so' (17:11). In Athens, the philosophers wanted to know 'what this new teaching is that you are presenting?' (17:19). In Corinth, 'he tried to persuade Jews and Greeks' (18:4) and was dragged before the tribunal, where the Jews said, 'This man is persuading the people to worship God' (18:13). For three months in the synagogue of Ephesus, he was 'reasoning and persuading them about the kingdom of God' (19:8) before 'reasoning daily' in the hall of Tyrannus for the next two years, enabling the whole of Asia Minor to hear the gospel (19:9,10). Luke vividly described the riot which eventually broke out among the silversmiths in

Ephesus. They said, 'this Paul has persuaded… a great many people, saying that gods made with hands are not gods.' (19:26)

Apollos had previously been at Ephesus, before helping the work in Corinth. We are told that he was an 'eloquent man' (18:24), who 'powerfully refuted the Jews in public, showing by the Scriptures that the Christ was Jesus' (18:28). King Festus shouted at Paul that he was mad, but Paul insisted that he was speaking 'true and rational words …the king knows about these things… For I am persuaded that none of these things has escaped his notice, for this has not been done in a corner' (26:25,26). And what did King Agrippa make of Paul's eloquent defence? 'In a short time would you persuade me to be a Christian?' (26:28)

The final picture we have of Paul is of him being under house arrest in Rome. We are told that great numbers came to his lodgings, where from morning to evening he tried 'to convince them about Jesus', and 'some were convinced by what he said, but others disbelieved … disagreeing among themselves' (28:23–25). There are then to my mind only two types of evangelism, persuasive evangelism and unpersuasive evangelism, and there is no point or purpose in being unpersuasive! Yet contemporary evangelism can rarely be described as 'arguing persuasively about the kingdom of God' (Acts 19:8 NIV).

We have looked at three areas to work on if we want to be Christian persuaders. We need to present our material attractively so that people can listen, explain our message carefully so that they can understand it, and address their questions and doubts so that they are convinced by the truth of what we are saying.

But being persuaded is not the whole story. They might conclude that Christianity is really true but want none of it!

I remember once holding a dialogue with students in a very packed room, with every inch of floor space covered. I had given a five-minute outline about Christian belief, and the ensuing discussion had lasted two hours and had gone well. As I drew the meeting to a close, summarising the implications of Christian belief, a student at the far end of the room got up to leave. He had to struggle to find floor space for each step of his way to the door. I stopped speaking and waited for this drama to end. Eventually he made it to the door which, because of the many bodies, was very difficult to open.

As he was about to leave, I broke the silence and asked, 'Can you tell us why you are leaving at this point?'

'Yes,' he said. 'I don't want anyone else to rule my life.' And with that he left.

That is, of course, the general state of humankind. It is the very definition of 'sin'. People do not want to let God be God over them. They would prefer the epitaph, 'I did it my way'.

So we also must pray that God would take these gospel truths, and not only give understanding and conviction of the truth of what we are saying, but by his Holy Spirit bring about that change of the heart, mind and will that will enable people to turn away from everything they know to be wrong and place their trust in Jesus as their Saviour, Lord and God. We must do our part in presenting the gospel persuasively, but only God can change their hearts.

CHAPTER 5
UNPERSUASIVE EVANGELISM

If there are only two types of evangelism – persuasive and unpersuasive – what does unpersuasive evangelism look like? There are various approaches today which fall a long way short of the way the apostles took the Gospel into the Greco-Roman world, and examining them will help us to see the differences between the two.

Presence

Some Christians today seem to think that the Gospel can be caught, rather like an infection! All you need to do is get close enough to people and the 'good news' will somehow rub off on them. Well, there is some truth in this. If we are living attractive and wholesome lives, people might want our company and even wonder what makes us tick. But if that occurs, they would then start asking questions, so we now are forced to move from presence to proclamation.

I was befriended by Christians in my teenage years. I particularly appreciated their kindness, humour and generous hospitality. They always made me welcome. At home, Mother found it stressful to entertain guests. In contrast, these folk were relaxed, welcoming and, importantly for a teenager, ready to share their food. They showed me the importance of hospitality in making friends.

As a result, I bought a modern translation of the New Testament, and without telling them, I read a chapter every night and repeated the process three times. Three years later, at 9.30p.m. on Tuesday, 17 May 1966, having resolved all my major questions about the general truth and integrity of the story (more on that in due course), and impressed by the way I saw it lived out in the lives of my friends, I committed my life to Christ. It was an eye-opening moment. Joy flooded my soul. Bursting with enthusiasm, I ran uphill all the way home to tell my father. He was singularly unimpressed, and for at least the next ten years believed I would grow out of it.

Presence alone, however, without learning the content of the good news, might actually give entirely the wrong impression. An optimistic humanist, believing in the essential goodness of human nature, might see the goodness and integrity of his friends as confirmation of his own atheism.

I am sure presence is more infectious when a non-Christian gets to know a group of Christians as I did. Being accepted by their group, l was able to learn all sorts of things about Christian attitudes, behaviour and beliefs. So, belonging often precedes believing, as long as the company of Christians is not silent! It is rather the persuasive context, where one can learn from both hearing discussion and observing behaviour over a prolonged period of time that has its powerful effect.

So, presence might lead to proclamation, but on its own, without verbal communication, it does not necessarily point to Christ. (This might say more about me than about you, but I have yet to find anyone so impressed by the sheer loveliness of my character that they have asked me for the secret of my inner spiritual beauty!)

If the sinless Christ did not adopt such an approach, and felt the need to teach as well as being good and kind, then so must we. His exemplary life was insufficient without words. If he needed to teach people about God, then surely we must give up on being silent witnesses.

Witness to personal experience

Once we open our mouths, we must decide what it is that we are going to bear witness to. For some people, they feel that they should talk about their own experience of God. Paul did this at times, talking about his conversion experience on the road to Damascus (Acts 22:6–11; 26:12–15). What was compelling about this was the dramatic change in his murderous character. The Christians weren't at all pleased to meet him when he arrived in Damascus. They saw him as a real threat, like meeting an ISIS jihadist (Acts 8:3; 9:1,13,14,21).

Your personal story is likely to be less dramatic than Paul's. In our culture, people might be quite pleased for you that you have had such a 'nice, comforting' subjective experience of God, and then share their own technique for calming down when they get stressed (perhaps by alcohol, music, meditation or shopping trips). People cannot enter into your experience to see what it is like from the inside. For this reason, I rarely talk about mine. Speaking only of your personal experience is anyway liable to say little about the objective Christ and a lot about you, none of which can be verified.

Proclamation

So I hope you agree with me that we need to tell people about Jesus, rather than about ourselves. Most Christians believe they need to both live consistent lives and also 'tell the old, old story'. The issue, then, is whether that is *all* we have to do – and I do not think it is. It is never enough *just* to tell the story. They need to be convinced that this story is actually true: Jesus not only lived in real history but we have reliable information about him. We are confident what he was like and we know what he taught. We have compelling evidence that Jesus spoke with authority and made extraordinary claims about himself, including having the audacity to forgive people their sins against God. These claims were necessarily either true or false. It is at this point that our story needs to be persuasive. Just telling people that Jesus died on a cross and rose from the dead is likely to be dismissed as foolishness. That is certainly what the Greek philosophers thought (1Corinthians 1:22,23; Acts 17:32)!

Monologue

Just telling the story will probably not be persuasive unless one faces head-on the objections that arise. One of the commonest objections concerns the Bible itself, because of the way the faith has been presented from the Bible. Christians believe the Bible to be the authoritative Word of God, but they should not expect unbelievers to accept it in the same way.

Commonly their underlying belief is that the Word of God speaks for itself. 'I would sooner defend a lion' they say, quoting Spurgeon. This nineteenth-century preacher is reported to have said:

> Open the door and let the lion out; he will take care of himself. Why, they are gone! He no sooner goes forth in his strength than his assailants flee. The way to meet infidelity is to spread the Bible. The answer to every objection against the Bible is the Bible.[9]

Of course, if the question is about the Bible, then answering from the Bible is entirely reasonable. If the question is a challenge to historic Christian belief, the same may apply. Even when the challenge comes from unbelievers, there are surely grounds for explaining carefully what the Bible says and does not say on the matter in order to answer their question.

However, those who quote Spurgeon in this context are being both naive and unbiblical. We have a detailed record as to how Paul used and quoted Scripture when evangelising Jews in Antioch (Acts 13:14–42). They already accepted the authority of Old Testament books. But this was hardly the way he addressed either the pagan farmers at Lystra (Acts 14:15–17) or the pagan philosophers in Athens (Acts 17:22–31). Yet these are the only two examples we have of Paul addressing non-Jews. Unlike the situation he found in the synagogues, neither the farmers nor the philosophers were remotely familiar with the Bible, nor had they any reason to accept its authority. So Paul made repeated assertions of biblical truths, which he cogently argued from 'authorities' in their own culture, which they did respect, arguing from nature in Lystra and from philosophy in Athens. He did not directly quote the Bible to them at all.

Simplistic techniques

The examples of evangelism in the New Testament show, in every case, that Jesus and his apostles did not learn evangelism by rote or follow a simplistic scheme. Rather they addressed individuals personally and tailor-made their presentations to the audience in question. They never thought for a moment that 'one size would fit all'. Most examples we have flow in the wake of a question. So Philip asked the Ethiopian eunuch, 'Do you understand what are you reading?' and allowed the Ethiopian to set the agenda (Acts 8:30–35).

Of course, it is much easier to have a pre-prepared statement to issue. But people are individuals. They all have varying degrees of knowledge, understanding and interest. We have to approach people as individuals, and progress at their pace.

This does put the onus on Christians to be constantly learning not only about their faith but also about the culture they live in, if they are to communicate effectively.

The need to listen

Dialogue has all too commonly been left out of the picture, yet Paul clearly engaged with the doubts and confusions of his hearers. He was listening to them and replying to them, whether in the synagogue or in the marketplace (Acts 17:17,18). Even his monologues were invariably followed by questions and debate.

Today, however, in reaction to the church's long tradition of monologue sermons, dialogue has been reduced to a specialised interfaith process, where all faiths are seen as equally valid and searching for similarities and common ground, rather than highlighting the differences and persuading people to change their minds.

Some radical theologians even go so far as to say that a relativist view of truth is an essential requirement for a person even to enter such a dialogue.[10] Paul Knitter made the self-refuting statement that 'we must be *absolutely* committed to positions that we know are *relative*'.[11] Well, that is not what the apostles were doing! We need to recapture their passion through persuasive dialogue to bring people to understanding and conviction of the truths of Christ – who, if he is whom he said he is, will one day hold us all to account.

As we have seen, we cannot separate proclamation from dialogue or reasoning. Our dialogue must engage with explanations and reasonable evidences which engage with the culture of our hearers in order to persuade them. That approach was normal evangelism for Paul.

The need to engage

Much evangelism fails because it does not engage with the world people live in. It seems irrelevant to them. As a result, it is boring and the audience falls asleep. As we shall see, the apostles engaged with their audience and directly addressed the pervading culture. Paul was so interesting that people wanted to hear more, not less. They weren't immediately agreeing with him, but they were riveted by what they heard.

So what then is apologetics?

The word '*apologia*' or '*apologeomai*' occurs some eighteen times in the New Testament, usually meaning 'an answer' and in a legal context, meaning a defence in response to accusations. So when Paul is pulled up before the authorities, be they tribunals, politarchs, proconsuls or kings, he gives an answer in defence of his beliefs and behaviour (see Acts 22:1; 25:16; 1 Corinthians 9:3; 2 Timothy 4:16).

The word only occurs three times in relation to the gospel. Two of these are in Philippians 1, but both occasions clearly have a legal ring to them, given that Paul is under house arrest in Rome because of the gospel: 'you are all partakers with me ... in the defence and confirmation of the gospel' (1:7), 'knowing that I am put here for the defence of the gospel' (1:16).

The best known reference is this: 'always being prepared to make a defence to anyone who asks you for a reason for the hope that is in you; yet do it with gentleness and respect' (1 Peter 3:15).

If people ask a question of you, it is rude not to answer them. But the church has latched on to the idea that the only place for reasoned argument is not in its general preaching but in response to specific intellectual questions from those who are inclined to ask them. A whole discipline of defensive 'apologetics' has been built on this basis. As one church report expressed it: 'On the whole apologists seek to remove obstacles in the minds of people *already attracted to faith*.'(Italics mine)[12]

But what if the person isn't interested in the Christian faith and isn't asking any questions? What if they are resting content in their pagan ideology? On this basis, should we leave them alone? Should we say nothing? If Paul had adopted such a perversion of the evangelistic task, would he have ever gone to Athens or Corinth – or indeed would he ever have left Jerusalem? He certainly did not go abroad by invitation! On that basis, he would only have spoken about Christ in response to enquiries. And that is where many Christians are today.

It is extraordinary that so much has been made of the discipline of Christian 'apologetics', when the word in the New Testament conveys little more than the word 'answer'. In fact, in my copy of a 1,356 page *Theological Dictionary of the New Testament*, which claims to cover 2,300 theologically significant New Testament words, 'apologia' is not one of them! Not a mention of it. This is because it is not a theologically significant word. Neither does the New Testament ever mention a breed of people in the early church called 'apologists'. That is not to say that Christians should not think carefully how they argue the case for Christ, but that they should not see it as a separate task from evangelism.

Now, it wouldn't matter if we had coined a new word which had a distinctive meaning and helped us think carefully about evangelism, but this word is a disaster. First of all, in the popular mind, it is assumed to be something to do with apologising, as though we should apologise for even mentioning the person of Jesus. Secondly, it sets up the intellect against a supposedly 'more spiritual' approach to evangelism – unargued, simple, monologue proclamation that is deaf to the cries of those who hear it.

What, then, are the features of 'unpersuasive' evangelism?

a) believing Christianity is caught but not taught;
b) witnessing to our subjective experience rather than the historic Christ;
c) simply informing people about the good news story;
d) assuming the authority of the Bible;

e) depending on simple techniques which are easily learned;

f) not listening to the views of unbelievers;

g) seeing dialogue as an activity for those who think that all truth is relative;

h) thinking it can be done by being boring and irrelevant;

i) seeing argument about truth as ungodly;

j) regarding persuasion as worldly power play;

k) seeing apologetics as a limited defensive strategy for helping enquiring intellectuals.

We need to get back to modelling our evangelism today on the rather more demanding example the apostles have given to us in the New Testament, where they persuaded people that what they were saying was actually true.

CHAPTER 6
PAUL AT ATHENS

———•———

In the opening paragraph of *Escape from Reason*, Francis Schaeffer's critique of twentieth-century culture, he wrote this:

> If a man goes overseas for any length of time, we would expect him to learn the language of the country to which he is going. More than this is needed, however, if he is really to communicate with the people among whom he is living. He must learn another language – that is the thought-forms of the people to whom he speaks. Only so will he have real communication with them and to them.[13]

When Paul went to Athens (see Acts 17:16-34), he clearly engaged with their thought-forms and beliefs, yet the charge is often made that Paul regretted this approach. His philosophical presentation to the Council of the Areopagus is said to have been 'unsuccessful'. Critics say that he had flattered their intellects and subsequently adopted a very different and more spiritual approach when he moved on to Corinth. His difficulties at Corinth are certainly intriguing, and we shall consider them shortly. But first, let us examine Luke's account of what happened when Paul spoke to the Athenian philosophers.

Tarsus

Paul was a Roman citizen, born in Tarsus, then the capital of the Roman province of Cilicia, in what is nowadays southern Turkey. This trading centre at the mouth of the river Cydnus is where Cleopatra met and captivated Mark Anthony in 41BC.

Plutarch described the extraordinary scene with multitudes lining the riverbanks as she sailed in, dressed as Venus reclining beneath a canopy of gold. Boys dressed as cupids cooled her with their fans, while silver oars dipped in time to the music of flutes, pipes and lutes.[14] It was also an important intellectual centre, with its own academy. Its library once held 200,000 books and the tutor to the Roman emperor Augustus studied there. By Paul's own account, Tarsus was 'no mean city' (Acts 21:39KJV).)!

We don't know when Paul left Tarsus but he probably began his classical education there, before completing it under Gamaliel in Jerusalem (Acts 22:3). It familiarised him with the teachings of both Epicurean and Stoic philosophers, which equipped him later to engage with the philosophers of Athens.[15]

A memorable event

Why should we believe that Luke presents anything like an accurate summary of Paul's address to the Council of the Areopagus? Firstly, this was not just another talk which Paul gave. This was special. Athens was the intellectual capital of the empire; it was the Oxford University of its day. Here was a strategic opportunity to speak to the movers and shakers of the academic world. Given such an opportunity to speak, who wouldn't remember what he had said? And Luke had plenty of opportunity to ask Paul about it. They sailed together to Rome, were shipwrecked on the island of Malta and had to spend the rest of the winter there (Acts 27:1 - 28:16). Knowing Paul would face trial in Rome, Luke would have been concerned to assemble documentation to be submitted in his defence – and the serious consideration he received at Athens might influence his reception in Rome.

Whether Paul was frogmarched from the Athenian marketplace to the Areopagus or had time to collect his thoughts, we do not know. Was he required to seek their approval of his teaching? There is no reference to formalities, a prosecutor, interrogation or a verdict. He seems to have been free to come or go.

Did he have a list of the key points he wished to present, scribbled on the 'back of an envelope', or whatever was the first-century equivalent of a postcard bought in the marketplace? Or did he just remember the headline issues subsequently? We shall unpack the content in a moment, but according to Luke, there were ten clear headings for his talk (Acts 17:22–31).

Paul's ten 'Bullet Points'

1) Introductory compliments v. 22
2) The unknown God v. 23
3) The transcendent Creator v. 24
4) The sustaining God v. 25
5) Human unity and equality v. 26
6) Seeking and finding v. 27
7) The immanence of God vv. 27,28
8) Man made in his likeness v. 29
9) Morally accountable v. 30

10) Righteous judgement by the risen Christ v. 31

Furthermore, the points that Luke recorded – and wrote as prose – are consistent with Paul's classical education, his theological writings (especially Romans 1–3), the record of his brief address to the pagan farmers of Lystra (Acts 14:14–18) and his deconstruction of ideas raised up against the knowledge of God at Corinth (2 Corinthians 10:5). In the light of these, the broad sweep of his Athenian address feels entirely right!

And let us also be clear that Luke makes no suggestion *at all* that Paul regretted his approach to the philosophers. Rather, he offers it as a classic example of Paul's preaching to non-Jews, a model for other Christians to emulate (which, indeed, they did). It is his only sermon addressed to non-Jews, which Luke outlined in careful detail. It is clearly not Luke's 'best guess' of what he thought Paul might have said.

That, anyway, is the natural reading of Acts. To imply that Luke recorded his synopsis of the Athenian speech as an example of how *not* to do evangelism – and then simply forgot to say so – makes Luke look very foolish. It is quite implausible. Surely, Luke intended this to be seen as a model example of how Paul addressed the pagan world.

The marketplace

Now we need to put this address into its context. Paul had already been engaging with both Epicurean and Stoic philosophers in the marketplace and the thrust of what he had been saying to them was focused on Jesus and the resurrection (Acts 17:18ff). This clearly intrigued them. They apparently thought he was advocating more foreign gods, like their popular god Isis from Egypt, and presumably two of them – 'Jesus' and 'Anástasis', where 'resurrection' was assumed to be a Greek name. And it was on this basis that they invited him to give a presentation of 'this new teaching' to the Council of the Areopagus. Here, Paul had the opportunity to give them an ordered presentation of his thinking.

We do not know how many people made up the council. If it was anything like the Roman senate, it would include philosophers, magistrates, lawyers, politicians, administrators and civic leaders. We don't know if this was a formal gathering or whether, like the Roman senate, it included a public audience. It seems that Dionysius was a council member and a woman named Damaris was also in attendance. Anyway, Paul addressed the assembly as 'People of Athens...'

To appreciate what Paul said, and how it engaged with his hearers, we need to understand a little of what the Epicureans and Stoics actually believed.

The Epicureans

Epicurus was a Greek philosopher who lived 300 years before Christ. Ethically, he was a 'consequentialist', believing good actions are ones that result in pleasure. This moral code allowed everyone to 'do their own thing' as long as it did not interfere with the happiness of others. People were free to make their own decisions on this basis. As this was their vision for the common good, Epicureans tended to be detached from wider society. They had a reputation for not caring about other people. They believed in gods who were remote and also didn't care, though they were critical of popular, superstitious religion. They did not need these gods and did not think the gods were at all interested in them. Death was the end. They did not believe anything followed it, so they would not be held to account for the way they lived. Consequently, there was nothing to fear – but there was also nothing to hope for. Life was a matter of chance and the aim was to enjoy it while it lasted or until your luck ran out.

The Stoics

Stoicism was propounded by Zeno, who lived at the same time as Epicurus. He saw the material world itself as having a 'soul' which determined, in a fatalistic way, the events of life. God was contained within creation and there was nothing of God outside of it. This 'pantheistic' view encouraged people to come to terms with the way the world is. Contentment could only be found in 'going with the flow' and accepting the way things were. This resulted in an emotionally detached rationalism, and there was no personal God to appeal to.

So both the Epicureans and the Stoics looked down upon the superstitious religious beliefs of the population at large. In modern terms, the Epicureans saw life as a lottery where you take your chances, while the Stoics were fatalists, seeing nature as an impersonal force which determines our destinies. The Epicureans focused on living for pleasure, while the Stoics gritted their teeth and accepted their fate. Superstition, chance and fatalism are common creeds all over the world today.

Paul's opening statements

If you have done any public speaking, you will know how important your opening sentences are. Will they engage with your listeners or antagonise them? Greek orators were expected to start with complimentary comments about each city they visited. Paul had been provoked by the idolatry he had observed in the city, and used that as his starting point, but in a positive way. Instead of attacking them, he affirms and commends them for their interest in religion. It was a tactful start, albeit with a hint of irony. He then skilfully gets underway using one of the objects of their worship, an altar he had observed 'To the unknown god'. This was a great introduction, because it was both intriguing and also underscored his central message that God has, in fact, made himself known.

Idolatry

But the God he was proclaiming was not a man-made god, who lived in a man-made temple. He did not need our help, protection or service. This is the God who made the entire world and everyone in it! He is entirely self-sufficient. He does not need us, but we are utterly dependent on him. This fundamentally inverted their viewpoint. We did not make him but he made us, giving us life, breath and everything. This was not just another demigod for their pantheon, but the God of all gods. Neither was he a regional god, such as Diana of the Ephesians, but the God of everyone because he created everyone.

Racism

This meant that all people in every nation have the same origin in creation. But this idea was contrary to their thinking, for the Athenians thought that they were a distinct and superior race, sprung from the soil of Attica, the peninsula of which Athens was the capital. Paul's God made every nation from a common ancestry, allocating their times and places – all the boundaries in which people live. As a result, everyone has an equal standing before God, who has no racial favourites.

Personal God

So Paul comes alongside their religiosity but distances himself from their central ideas. The reason God made people was not that they might serve him 'as if he needed anything'. They were right to be religious but this inner yearning was given for a purpose – that they might seek after God and personally come to know him. This God of gods, unlike the pantheistic view of the Stoics, is personal and transcends everything he has created. Yet he is not remote. Contrary to the Epicurean view, which held that God was unapproachable, unknowable and disinterested, he is immanent, meaning that he is very close to each of us. Paul illustrated this, not by quoting the Old Testament (such as Isaiah 57:15) but by quoting a poem by Epimenides of Crete (c.600BC), 'For in him we live and move and have our being.'

Made in his likeness

Paul now makes an appeal to our divine origins. We come from God, God does not come from us nor is he to be found in the material world. 'As some of your own poets have said, "We are indeed [God's] offspring."' Instead of quoting Genesis 1, Paul quotes from the Stoic poet Aratus, who lived around 300BC, although it may have had a pantheistic meaning for the Greeks. Paul uses it as a stepping stone to confront them with the absurdity of thinking that God is a figment of artistic imagination, like the gold, silver or stone gods that he found all over the city. Not only were these gods made by the art and craft of human design, but the superstitious Greeks believed that the gods became embodied in their artwork and empowered it. As a result it was common for Roman homes across the Greco-Roman empire to have shrines, often with statuettes in miniature temples, at which the owners would pray each day. Gods are not made by people in human likeness, but the creator God made people in his divine likeness. We bear the family resemblance of God. We are his offspring, not the other way around. Their idolatry was the product of ignorance, and the God Paul proclaims calls everyone to turn away from such wilful foolishness and humble themselves before their Creator, who will also be their judge.

Moral awareness

Did Paul really introduce the concept of judgement so abruptly? This was surely another 'bullet point' heading that he reported to Luke. Presumably Paul would have developed the idea of us being God's offspring along the lines of the opening chapters of his letter to the Romans (see Romans 1:28 – 2:16). This would have highlighted the moral otherness of God, revealed to human conscience. He shows no favouritism but calls everyone in every nation to turn away from both folly and wickedness. Why? Because God has revealed himself in the righteous person of Christ, whom he has appointed to be our judge and has assured us of this by raising him from the dead.

Had Paul finished or was he prevented from saying anymore? Presumably there was a great deal he could have said about Christ if he had had the opportunity. It is difficult to imagine that he mentioned the resurrection without describing Christ's death for our sins, which Paul understood to be of central importance (1 Corinthians 15:3-5). Luke's account suggests that the meeting broke up, not because he spoke of Christ's death, but because of Paul's claim that God had raised him from the dead.

Judgement

This idea that God will judge the world in righteousness was an altogether novel concept for Greek minds to contemplate. The myths surrounding the Greek gods suggest there was hardly a kind or righteous thought to be found among them. Violent, jealous, greedy and capricious, they inflicted their hatred upon one another in the most unpredictable and shocking manner. There was no integrity, consistency or justice to be found among them. They sulked and schemed against each other and performed the most spiteful revenge. Paul was proclaiming a God who was quite unlike any of the Greek gods. Here was a loving God of upright, consistent moral character, who will call us all to account and judge the entire world with justice. And if we want to know what he is like, we must look at the moral stature of the 'man he has appointed' to carry out that judgement. If we want to know where we stand before God, we must look long and hard into the face of Jesus Christ.

The fallout

We don't know how long Paul took to unpack these great truths, summarised by Luke in just a few sentences, but his audience had had to come a very long way in a short time! They did not believe that the gods, which they represented with their own artistic skills, had created the universe, nor were they paragons of virtue. They believed that Mother Earth had arisen out of a dark void and created the gods. Now Paul was calling them to face the true and the living God, who created the earth and everything in it, who was calling them all to repentance and faith because they faced a just and righteous judgement before Christ.

These new ideas were quite radical. Not surprisingly, some mocked him, others wanted to hear more, but some believed him and became Christians that day. Here was a stunning address, sensitively shaped for his audience, drawing on Paul's knowledge of their culture, philosophy and literature, engaging deeply with Greek thought but faithfully proclaiming the risen Christ. It was real communication in language they understood.

'But surely,' the critics say, 'the results speak for themselves. Hardly anyone was converted at Athens. In fact, they ridiculed him.' (Acts 17:32)

It is true that his message met with mixed results; it always does! It did so in Iconium, Lystra, Thessalonica, Corinth and Ephesus (Acts 14:4-6; 14:19; 17:5; 18:2; 19:23ff). Same message – same results. In Athens, some mocked him – but others were keen to ask him back. 'We want to hear you again on this subject', they said. I have given some pretty awful talks in my life, but when I get invited back, I assume the previous one must have gone down rather well. Furthermore, if I had been bored or irritated by someone else's talk, the last thing I would do is to invite him back. That is like saying, 'Hit me again, please!'

But while some were interested in Paul's address, an unknown number of others were clearly converted, two of whom Luke names. There would be little point in naming them if Luke's readers had never heard of them. The implications are that Dionysius the Areopagite and the woman Damaris were either notable figures in Athens or became prominent workers in the church. Dionysius was probably both those things. Writing 250 years later, Roman historian Eusebius records that Dionysius became the first Bishop of Athens. If that is true, it would justify Luke in recording his name.

Three groups of people, the pantheistic Stoics, the pleasure-seeking Epicureans and the superstitious populace heard Paul's presentation of the Christian God. It engaged with, and yet profoundly disturbed, each of them. Paul did not quote the Bible to them; it was an authority they did not recognise. They were inevitably ignorant of the Hebrew Scriptures and had no access to them. Yet, drawing on their own knowledge of humanity and culture, Paul proclaimed the God revealed in Christ and the Hebrew Scriptures. His audience then fell into three very different groups, each presumably a mixture of the initial groups, some of whom mocked, some of whom wanted to hear more and some of whom became Christians.

Then Paul moved on to Corinth.

CHAPTER 7
WHATEVER HAPPENED IN CORINTH?

———•———

When I came to you, brothers, I did not come with eloquence or superior wisdom as I proclaimed to you the testimony about God. For I resolved to know nothing while I was with you except Jesus Christ and him crucified. I came to you in weakness and fear, and with much trembling. My message and my preaching were not with wise and persuasive words, but with a demonstration of the Spirit's power, so that your faith might not rest on men's wisdom, but on God's power.
The apostle Paul (1 Corinthians 2:1–5, NIV 1984)

So Paul described his arrival in Corinth. As a result, some have suggested that after Athens, he radically changed his approach from an intellectual one to a spiritual and unargued presentation of the gospel. How, then, are we to understand this apparent change? What did he mean when he said he avoided eloquence, wisdom and persuasive words? Why was he 'resolved to know nothing while I was with you except Jesus Christ and him crucified'?

And what was he so frightened about that he arrived in Corinth in 'fear, and … much trembling'? This Paul had been hauled up before the authorities time and again. He had faced jealous mobs which drove him out of Antioch; he fled from Iconium to Lystra to avoid being stoned to death – only to be stoned when he got there! He was dragged out of that city half-dead. He sailed on to Macedonia where he received a sound beating before being thrown into a prison, which then collapsed in an earthquake. He was subsequently attacked by a rabble in Thessalonica, those 'lewd fellows of a baser sort' (KJV), who pursued him to Berea, from whence he escaped to Athens (Acts 13:44 – 17:15).

Now he comes to Corinth and has an attack of nerves? If he was going to have a nervous breakdown, surely he would have done that a long time ago! This story doesn't seem to add up. There must be more going on here than is apparent.

The 'hermeneutic' challenge

Trying to understand any ancient document throws up the immediate question as to what the words meant to the writer at that time and how he wanted them to be understood by his original readers. We have to try to understand them first in the context of those original 'horizons', before we can jump the centuries – and the cultures – and apply them within our own 'horizons'.

This passage of 1 Corinthians 2:1–5 throws up enough *red alert* lights to suggest there is something important going on here that is not immediately obvious to us, reading it some 2,000 years later. So we have to do some digging!

Some have thought that the background situation at Corinth was the rise of Gnosticism, but there seems to be no evidence of that anywhere before the second century. Others have thought the Corinthians were just a particularly divisive and contentious lot. Again, some have thought that the use of rhetoric in Corinth was the problem, while others have felt they were just arrogant and that Paul's eloquence did not measure up to their Greco-Roman standards.

While Paul's statements in 1 Corinthians 2:1–5 have led some to the idea that Paul changed his evangelistic strategy in Corinth, it soon becomes apparent that these same ill-defined difficulties are behind much that Paul has written.

A growing list

What was going on with the divisions which were reported by 'Chloe's household', such that some say, 'I follow Paul' or 'I follow Apollos' and 'I follow Cephas [Peter]'? What was all the fuss about baptism, such that Paul was grateful he had only baptised a few individuals? And how did all this rivalry relate to his comment that he did not preach 'with words of eloquent wisdom' (1 Corinthians 1:10–17)?

And how come 'his speech [was] of no account' (2 Corinthians 10:10)? Why did he write, 'Even if I am unskilled in speaking, I am not so in knowledge' (2 Corinthians 11:6), when we know his preaching was highly effective and his word skills were very impressive?

When gazing at the night sky, as your eyes adapt, more and more stars come into view. So it is here: the more you look, the greater is the complexity of what you see.

Who, then, were the 'debater[s] of this age' who were seen to be foolish in the light of Paul's preaching (1 Corinthians 1:20, 21)? And who were the 'wise', when God 'catches the wise in their craftiness', and whose thoughts were 'futile' (1 Corinthians 3:19,20).

Why was money such a touchy issue? '… the Lord commanded

that those who proclaim the gospel should get their living by the gospel. But I have made no use of any of these rights, nor am I writing these things to secure any such provision'(1 Corinthians 9:14,15).Why did Paul feel he should pay his way by making tents in Corinth (Acts 18:3; 1 Corinthians 4:12)?

And what was the recurring significance of 'flattery' and 'greed', which spills over into letters to other destinations. 'We never came with words of flattery, nor with a pretext for greed' he wrote to the Thessalonians (1 Thessalonians 2:5). Who on earth would have thought that he might have come in that way?

He also wrote to Rome about 'those who cause divisions' who 'serve ... their own appetites, and by smooth talk and flattery deceive the hearts of the naïve' (Rom 1:17,18).

Another thread is the accusation that Paul was physically weak. 'God chose what is weak in the world to shame the strong' (1 Corinthians 1:27). 'I was with you in weakness' (1 Corinthians 2:3) and 'they say... his bodily presence is weak' (2 Corinthians 10:10). How come they thought he looked weak? Given all he had endured, he can hardly have been physically fragile!

And what are we to make of the implied social class distinctions: 'not many of you were wise according to worldly standards, not many were powerful, not many of noble birth. But God chose what is foolish...what is weak...what is low and despised in the world, even things that are not, to bring to nothing the things that are, so that no human being might boast in the presence of God' (1Corinthians 1:26–29). Paul's tent making was a lowly trade. There is rather a lot about boasting: 'If I must boast, I will boast of the things that show my weakness' (2Corinthians 11:30). 'Not that we dare to...compare ourselves with some of those who are commending themselves ... we will not boast ... We do not boast... "Let the one who boasts, boast in the Lord", he wrote

(2 Corinthians 10:12–17). Who were 'these super-apostles', who looked down upon Paul (2 Corinthians 11:5)?

So what started off as just five verses (1Corinthians 2:1–5) which are difficult to interpret, now appears to be part of a major undercurrent with a dozen different features, having extensive repercussions for Paul's engagement with the Greco-Roman world.

Sophistic oratory

Antony Thistleton, in his magisterial commentary on 1 Corinthians, writes of 'The explosion of recent work on rhetoric in the Greco-Roman world and in Paul'.[16] He accepts a growing consensus that a certain type of Roman oratory (known as the 'Second Sophistic') explains a very great deal. In fact, it appears to be the elephant in the room!

Chief protagonist in this has been Dr Bruce Winter, formerly

 warden of Tyndale House, Cambridge and director of the Institute of Early Christianity in the Greco-Roman World. His book, *Philo and Paul among the Sophists* sets out the case.[17] In the preface, G.W. Bowersock, professor of Ancient History at Princeton, writes 'Through his mastery of both New Testament scholarship and Roman history, Bruce Winter has succeeded in documenting, for the first time, the Sophistic movement of the mid-first century.'[18]

Drawing on the writings of Philo, a first-century Jew in Alexandria (20BC– AD50) as well as the Greek 'Second Sophistic' orator, philosopher and writer Dio Chrysostom (AD40–115), the Roman historian Plutarch (AD46–120) and

others, Winter compares them with the observations Paul made following his visit to Corinth. This has enabled him to establish that the Sophistic orators were an active force in those two major Mediterranean cities, both centres of commerce and education in the middle of the first century AD. Indeed, the first four chapters of 1 Corinthians appear to be a critique of the Second Sophistic movement.

The first Sophists were philosophers at the height of the Greek civilisation, but education and philosophy fell into decline. Under the Roman Empire, the Greeks sought to recover their heritage and the glories of their past. This Second Sophistic movement was thought to have begun towards the end of the first century AD, from the time of Nero, surviving until the middle of the third century AD. Winter has shown that this timeframe must now be extended earlier.

Two schools

There were two main schools in the revival of Sophistic oratory. The more philosophical and traditional school (the Atticist) was based in Athens. However, it is the Asianic school, originating and functioning outside of Athens, which seems to have given the movement its bad reputation. Philostratus, a Sophist writing in the third century, described it as being 'flowery, bombastic, full of startling metaphors, too metrical, too dependent on tricks of rhetoric, too emotional'.[19] He called it 'theatrical shamelessness'.[20]

As we have seen, there are two kinds of rhetoric – the good and the bad! Aristotle had defined three modes of persuasion: *ethos* (the credibility of the speaker), *pathos* (the disposition of the audience) and *logos* (the clarity of the argumentation). In order to be persuasive, an argument needs to be sound (good *logos*), but the speaker needs to be respected enough for people to listen to him (good *ethos*), while the audience needs to be interested in what he is saying (good *pathos*).[21] There is nothing sub-Christian in any of that. These are proper rhetorical considerations for any speaker to reflect upon. Good rhetoric is all about good communication.

The problem comes when the speaker makes himself out to be something he is not (bad *ethos*), adopts a careless approach to truth (bad *logos*) and makes his primary appeal only to the emotions (bad *pathos*), so that his performance becomes more important than his message.

Some people are very gifted communicators. Their voices and demeanour are attractive. They have what the Irish call the 'gift of the gab' and could sell a second-hand car to anyone! These Sophist orators were so good they performed professionally. They were not philosophers so much as travelling exhibitionists, who went from city to city to entertain the people with their rhetorical skills. Paul, in contrast, 'wants to let truth speak for itself, not to manipulate rhetoric to sway his audience'.[22]

Paul wrote of his own ministry (concerning *ethos*, *logos* and *pathos*): 'we have renounced disgraceful, underhanded ways. We refuse to practice cunning or to tamper with God's word, but by the open statement of the truth we would commend ourselves to everyone's conscience in the sight of God' (2 Corinthians 4:2). But that, it seems, is the opposite of what the Sophist orators excelled in.

Roman education

I recently heard a university vice-chancellor saying that he thinks every one of his students should be taught the art of public speaking. This is an essential skill, in his view, for all senior posts, whether academic or commercial. Well, the Romans evidently agreed with him. Training in eloquence was an essential part of their further education, learning not just the rudiments of philosophy but appropriate rhetorical skills.

Every educated person of high rank in Roman society, whether senators, ambassadors, politicians, administrators, poets, magistrates, diplomats or soldiers, was trained in rhetoric. This was a skill of the educated upper classes in contrast with the Christians of whom 'not many ... were wise according to worldly standards ... powerful ...[or] of noble birth' (1 Corinthians 1:26). In comparison, they were the 'foolish' things which 'shame the wise... [the] things that are not, to bring to nothing things that are' (1 Corinthians 1:27,28).

What, then, were the features of this particular Asianic style of Sophist oratory?

The Asianic Sophists

These Sophists were celebrity speakers who travelled from city to city. They always charged fees and made their living from their oratory. The best earned a fortune and some became major benefactors to the cities they visited. Paul, in contrast, was not a pedlar of God's Word for profit but saw himself as commissioned by God, not the people (2 Corinthians 2:17).

There were established conventions surrounding the arrival of an orator. Their initial 'coming' to town was important and followed a set pattern. There was advance publicity, and venues such as amphitheatres or lecture halls were booked. There was a sense of expectation in the crowd, who looked to be entertained – and the orator's initial reception determined his future.

Orators were expected to begin with an introductory speech (an *encomium*) where they would say flattering things about the city and its people (see Acts 17:22). They may also have made

generous gifts to the city. Depending on how well this was received, they could then speak on a wide range of topics, often determined in advance but sometimes chosen by the audience at the time, giving the orator only a few minutes in which to gather his thoughts. He might be asked to describe an historic or fictional event, such as the death of a Greek hero. This would allow him to describe the scene dramatically, pulling on the heartstrings of the audience. He would look for loud applause and shouts of acclamation from the crowd, as he basked in his own glory. 'Dio states that they are as ineffectual as eunuchs. They love their reputation and so never say anything to offend their audience: thus they simply expound the views of their hearers', writes Winter.[23]

Their appearance was very important. Many were fit and athletic, having trained in the gymnasium. Some were described as 'gorgeous peacocks'.[24] They appeared in elaborate and effeminate dress, with coiffured hair-dos. They might pluck their body hair[25] and wear expensive jewellery. Their affected manner extended to a sing-song voice, with 'charming pronunciations' and rhythmic metres in their speech. They displayed expressive glances and theatrical gestures, stomping their feet and falling to their knees, then pausing for applause and shouts of approval.

Winter quotes Philostratus, who noted that when Alexander of Seleucia came to Athens his 'perfect elegance' sent an appreciative murmur through the crowd. He was described as 'godlike' – 'for his beard was curly and of moderate length, his eyes large and melting, his nose well-shaped, his teeth very white, his fingers long and slender and well-fitted to hold the reins of eloquence'.[26]

Their rhetorical flow of words was everything – while truth counted for nothing. This was a style of entertainment, equivalent in its day to the music halls of the nineteenth century, or the pop stars and *Strictly Come Dancing* of today. The crowds knew what to expect – and they expected to be amused, emotionally moved and generally uplifted.

The Corinthian audience clearly had expectations of Paul that he would never satisfy. Paul wrote, 'When I came to you, I did not come with eloquence or human wisdom' (1 Corinthians 2:1NIV).He was not letting them nominate the subject matter but had resolved 'to know nothing while I was with you except Jesus Christ and him crucified' (1 Corinthians 2:2 NIV). He had no intention of speaking about Greek myths! Neither was he giving a rehearsed performance with dramatic gestures, flowing rhetoric and staged pauses. Preaching for Paul was in 'plain style', drawing attention to Christ and not to himself (an example for all modern preachers). He was reliant on the Spirit's power, not human cleverness.

Thistleton comments:

...what we now know of the rhetorical background at

Corinth, releases Paul of any hint of an uncharacteristic or obsessional anti-intellectualism, or any lack of imagination or communicative flexibility. His settled resolve was that he would do only what served the gospel of Christ crucified, regardless of people's expectations or seductive shortcuts to success, most of all the seduction of self-advertisement. Neither then nor now does the gospel rest on the magnetism of 'big personalities'.[27]

The Sophistic orators each cultivated a following of 'disciples' and there was great rivalry between performers, sometimes descending into physical violence between their supporters. These disciples would imitate their heroes, mimicking their accents, their walks and their attire. This gives a context for understanding why Paul wrote, 'I urge you, then, be imitators of me' (1 Corinthians 4:16).

There was a long history of this rivalry. Dio reported that back in the days of Diogenes in the fourth century BC:

> One could hear crowds of wretched sophists around Poseidon's temple shouting and reviling one another, their disciples, as they were called, fighting one another, many reading aloud their stupid works, many poets reciting their poems while others applauded them... and pedlars not a few, peddling whatever they happened to have.[28]

Paul's contemporary Philo, the Alexandrian Jew, described the Sophists as 'imposters, flatterers, inventors of cunning plausibilities, who know well how to cheat and mislead, but that only, and have no thought for honest truth'.[29]

Speaking to a huge crowd in Alexandria, Greek philosopher

Dio Chrysostom accused the orators of deception, 'If in the guise of philosophers they do these things [declaim their speeches] with a view to their own profit and reputation and not to improve you, that is indeed shocking.' They cared nothing about their audiences. Dio went on to compare them with visiting physicians, who instead of providing treatment for the sick, bring only flowers and perfume![30]

An even earlier example of this style of oratory is described by the Roman historian Plutarch in relation to Cleopatra's Mark Anthony (83–30BC). He 'devoted himself to military training and to the study of public speaking, adopting what was known as the Asianic style. This type of oratory...had much in common with Anthony's own mode of life, which was boastful, insolent, and full of empty bravado and misguided aspirations.'[31]

This sense of bravado draws attention to Paul's comments about fear and trembling. Thistleton comments that this phrase contrasts with 'the self-confident, self-promotion of the sophist's visit. Paul is precisely not a visiting orator come to entertain the crowds as an audience-pleasing performer.'[32]

The importance of the arrival of the orator in a city is touched on by Paul, distancing himself from such expectations: 'When I came to you...I did not come with eloquence.'(1 Corinthians 2:1NIV). Paul must have been a colossal disappointment to them!

Lampooning the Sophists

Lucian of Samosata, a second-century rhetorician, wrote a satire called *Dialogues of the Dead*. Lampooning the Sophists, he describes the Olympian god Hermes welcoming the soul of a 'philosopher' on board his boat to be transported across the Styx to Hades:

My goodness, what a bundle: quackery, ignorance, quarrelsomeness, vainglory, idle questioning, prickly arguments, intricate conceptions, humbug, and gammon and wishy-washy hair-splittings without end; and hullo! Why, here's avarice and self-indulgence, and impudence! Luxury, effeminacy and peevishness! Yes, I see them all and you need not try to hide them. Away with falsehood and swagger and superciliousness; why, the three-decker is not built that would hold you with all this luggage![33]

And that, it seems, is what Paul had to compete with at Corinth!

Rereading the text

So now review those words of 1Corinthians 2:1–5, here in a translation offered by Anthony Thistleton:[34]

1) As for me, when I came to you, brothers and sisters, I did not come with high-sounding rhetoric or a display of cleverness in proclaiming to you the mystery of God.
2) For I did not resolve to know anything to speak among you except Jesus Christ and Christ crucified.
3) I came to you in weakness, with much fear and trembling.
4) My speech and my proclamation were not with enticing, clever words, but by transparent proof brought home powerfully by the Holy Spirit,
5) that your faith should not rest on human cleverness, but on God's power.

Winter says that these verses reveal 'a distinct constellation of rhetorical terms and allusions'.[35] They reflect the extraordinary cultural context in which Paul was working, and not some change of strategy on his part to avoid engaging with philosophical ideas.

Finally, with the curtain being drawn back on the Sophist orators, we might now see some of Paul's statements to the Thessalonians in a new light. Paul wrote this during his time in Corinth around AD51:

- 1:5: 'our gospel came to you not only in word, but also in power and in the Holy Spirit and with full conviction. You know what kind of men we proved to be among you for your sake. And you became imitators of us and of the Lord...'
- 1:9: 'For they themselves report concerning the kind of reception we had among you...'
- 2:1–9: '...our coming to you was not in vain... For our appeal does not spring from error or impurity or any attempt to deceive...so we speak, not to please man, but to please God... For we never came with words of flattery, as you know, nor with a pretext for greed – God is witness. Nor did we seek glory from people, whether from you or from others, though we could have made demands as apostles of Christ. But we were gentle among you, like a nursing mother taking care of her own children...ready to share … not only the gospel of God but also our own selves, because you had become very dear to us. For you remember, brothers, our labour and toil: we worked night and day, that we might not be a burden to any of you, while we proclaimed to you the gospel of God.'

In conclusion

It has been suggested by many people over the years that Paul, disappointed by the reception he had at Athens, changed his approach when he moved on to Corinth.[36] In Athens, he seemed to argue from Greek culture and natural theology (in creation, human nature and conscience) quoting from Greek writers (Epimenides of Crete and Aratus of Cilicia) rather than Scripture, to address the philosophers. So some had assumed that it was this philosophic style of 'eloquence or superior wisdom' (1 Corinthians 2:1 NIV), which he now abandoned.

However, there is nothing in Luke's writing to suggest a change of tack. His description of Paul's strategy in Corinth (Acts 18) is very similar to the descriptions of Paul in Thessalonica and Athens beforehand and in Ephesus subsequently (Acts 17, 19).

As for the place and style of argument in his presentation, it was to the Corinthians, not the Athenians that he wrote, 'The weapons of our warfare are not of the flesh but have divine power to demolish strongholds. We demolish arguments and every lofty opinion raised against the knowledge of God, and we take every thought captive to obey Christ' (2 Corinthians 10:4,5).

If he had a rough time in Athens, he certainly had difficulties in Corinth, which have previously been difficult to understand. I have listed at least a dozen such 'mysteries' from the text of Paul's letters. Occam's razor encourages us to look for a single solution rather than a range of explanations to solve a complex problem. We have such an explanation here. The oratory of the Asianic Sophists, so different from that of the Athenian Sophists, has now been shown to have been a major feature of Corinthian life at the time of Paul's visit. It has ample power to explain both the depths of Paul's difficulty and the scope of the wide-ranging details he has given us.

The idea that Paul changed his tactics in Corinth and abandoned cultural and persuasive arguments in his preaching must now be laid to rest. We have here an altogether more compelling account of the difficulties he faced.

CHAPTER 8
APPEALING TO NATURE

—— · ——

A few years ago, I organised what I hoped would be a debate on Islam. A leading British Muslim agreed to take part and debate with Professor Gary Habermas. The Muslim agreed to promote the meeting and promised that many Muslims would attend. In the event, he came alone with his driver and seemingly no other Muslim attended. Gary Habermas spoke first and presented his well-known arguments concerning the earliest evidence for Christianity, focusing on the historicity of Paul's credal statement in 1 Corinthians 15:3–5.[37] It was a powerful case, tracing the beliefs 'of first importance', concerning Christ's death and resurrection, on sound, documented, historical evidence back to within three to five years of the events themselves.

How would his opponent respond? Well, he didn't. He engaged with none of the issues and offered no arguments at all to support his views. He merely stated his Islamic beliefs, interspersed with such phrases as, 'We are taught to believe this...', 'We are told that...'. No justification of these Koranic beliefs was made at any point. His presentation was entirely 'fideistic', that is, a statement of faith, unargued and unengaged with any contrary opinion. Personally, I found it shocking. This did not even follow the rules of polite conversation, where you would respond to what the other person has just said. There was no exchange. It was as if Habermas had said nothing.

The fideism of Karl Barth

However, fideism is not confined to Muslims. The greatest Protestant theologian of the twentieth century adopted entirely this approach. Karl Barth did not believe in arguments or evidences to proclaim Christianity, and his influence persists strongly today. Such rational approaches to belief could in his view do nothing to facilitate a personal encounter with Christ. The evidence of nature and apologetic reasoning had no role in bringing people to faith.

In his view, such rational thought could only benefit those who already believed in God, and such belief could only come about by God's revelation of himself. It cannot justify itself through external criteria. The argument he proposed went entirely one way – from God to the world and not from the world of human thought and experience towards God. Here is the antithesis of dialogue. God's revelation must be accepted by faith, unaided by reason, whether historical, scientific, cultural, moral, psychological or social. Such fields of discourse do not overlap at any point with Barthian biblical theology.

In so doing, Barth broke free from the long Christian tradition that God has revealed himself as the ultimate author of two books, Scripture and nature; in what he has said and in what he has done. Needless to say, his approach plays straight into the hands of the New Atheists, who keep asserting that faith is a blind leap, unrelated to evidence. Endorsing such a view leaves us with no stepping stones from our common experience. We are left with a take-it-or-leave-it, undiscussable, theological imperialism, whose truth claims must be accepted uncritically, lock, stock and barrel. This leap of faith is, of course, the same for all cults and religions including Islam, whose beliefs are walled off from intellectual enquiry and justification.

It also plays into the hands of relativists, who maintain that the truth they have found is their own personal truth – 'it is true for me'. Keith Ward has written that adding those two little words 'for me' is 'a central heresy of our culture'.[38] It is the ultimate denial of 'public truth', that reality which is objectively true for everyone, whether or not you believe it or like it. And it plays into the hands of those for whom subjective experience is the final arbiter of truth, leaving them at the mercy of another experience. Such theology, being undiscussable, loses all pretensions to be an academic discipline with a rightful place in university life.[39]

Barth's historical context

Barth's approach was certainly extreme but, not surprisingly, it had an historical context. Barth was born in 1886 and was initially trained in Protestant Liberalism. He came to see that this human-centred approach to theology was too deeply immersed in German culture and he countered it in his preaching by emphasising Christ-centred, biblical theology. Matters came to a head when his former university teachers declared their support for German warmongering under Kaiser Bill.

The subsequent rise of Nazism between the wars led Barth to draw up the Barmen Declaration of the Confessing Church in 1934, which said:

We reject the false doctrine, as though the Church could and would have to acknowledge as a source of its proclamation, apart from and besides this one Word of God, still other events and powers, figures and truths, as God's revelation... as though there were areas of our life in which we would not belong to Jesus Christ...as though the Church were permitted to abandon the form of its message...to changes in prevailing ideological and political convictions.[40]

These were certainly heady days. An extreme theology came out of extreme circumstances! Natural theology, being linked with German national *volk*-religion, was set against the revealed religion of Christ in Scripture, and Barth's theology became all the more extreme in its defence. His biblical theology became isolated from rationality, presupposing its own truth, which needed no justification. He maintained that God in his sovereignty makes himself knowable. Humanity in its sinfulness cannot otherwise obtain any knowledge of God. A great gulf is fixed, bridged only by God in disclosing himself in Christ through the work of the Holy Spirit. Such knowledge is entirely a work of grace, unaided by human intellect.

Responding to fideism

What, then, can one say in response to such biblical fideism? Well, you could say it is self-defeating, as it denies rational justification for its beliefs. Why, then, should anyone believe it? As rational beings, we demand rational justification for what we believe. It is essential to our humanity; it is a God-like property marking us out from other animals.

We might also say that it is particularly attractive to the intellectually lazy or timid, who cannot be bothered to answer people's rational objections to faith. Such fragility is common. People justify their belief in Christ through their belief in the Bible, and justify their belief in the Bible through Christ's teaching. As we have seen, this argument is entirely circular and closed off from debate. Evangelism is made easy, believing that only God can open blind eyes and that we have no role in this. We can 'tell' others about the gospel, and if they don't grasp it, we can only tell them again, perhaps more loudly. This may be a caricature of what happens but, I suggest, it is close enough to the truth to be immediately recognisable. For many orthodox Christians, it justifies a 'simple proclamation' approach to evangelism, devoid of any need to persuade.

Is it biblical?

More importantly, however, and somewhat ironically, we must accuse Barth's biblicism of being unbiblical! The Scriptures themselves testify to the validity of human rationality and they encourage rational thought about the world we live in. They assert there is a knowledge of God to be found in the world he has created. '"Come now, let us reason together," says the LORD' (Isaiah 1:18).

So the psalmist tells us that, 'The heavens declare the glory of God, and the sky above proclaims his handiwork... Their voice goes out through all the earth, and their words to the end of the world' (Psalm 19:1,4).

The apostle Paul quotes this verse in his letter to the Romans: 'So faith comes by hearing, and hearing through the word of Christ. But I ask, have they not heard? Indeed they have, for "Their voice has gone out to all the earth, and their words to the ends of the world"' (Rom 10:17,18).

In other words, the glory of God can be seen through what

he has made, and that declaration of God is made to everyone. Again in Psalms 8 and 104, the writers say that when they look at the work of God's hands, they draw theological conclusions about the majesty of God and the dominion of humanity over God's abundant provision in nature.

This surely must have been in Paul's thinking when he wrote that what can be known about God is evident even to sinful people, who suppress the truth by their wickedness.

> For what can be known about God is plain to them, because God has shown it to them. For his invisible attributes, namely, his eternal power and divine nature, have been clearly perceived, ever since the creation of the world, in the things that have been made. So they are without excuse. For although they knew God, they did not honour him as God or give thanks to him, but they became futile in their thinking, and their foolish hearts were darkened. (Romans 1:19–21)

Here surely is a very clear mandate for appealing to what is called 'general revelation' or 'natural theology'. And if this were not true, how would Old Testament figures such as Abraham have ever believed in God, such that they recognised his call long before any Scriptures were written?

As atheist and *Times* columnist Matthew Parris has written:

> Because inbred in me and all humans is an inescapable feeling that what comes after us matters; that legacy matters, that what we do, what we build, how we live our lives and what we leave behind, is important to us now, though we shall be oblivious to it then...This is the eternal clash between simple observation – that for each of us everything is coming to an

end – and one of our deepest instincts: that this cannot be all there is...There has to be something: we feel it in our very marrow.[41]

Preaching to pagans

This testimony in nature is used by Paul in his evangelistic preaching to the pagan farmers at Lystra:

> you should turn from these vain things to a living God, who made the heaven and earth and the sea and all that is in them. In past generations he allowed all the nations to walk in their own ways. Yet he did not leave himself without witness, for he did good by giving you rains from heaven and fruitful seasons, satisfying your hearts with food and gladness.
> (Acts 14:15–17)

Here Paul appeals to the ordering of nature and its generous provision, which should have been seen for what it was, causing people to give thanks to their Creator, on whom they were dependent. He takes up this theme again with the philosophers at Athens:

> What … you worship as unknown, this I proclaim to you. The God who made the world and everything in it, being Lord of heaven and earth...gives to all mankind life and breath and everything... that they should seek God, in the hope that they might feel their way towards him and find him.

He then appeals to their own natures. 'Being then God's offspring, we ought not to think that the divine being is like gold or silver or stone, an image formed by the art and imagination of man.

The times of ignorance God overlooked, but now he commands all people everywhere to repent...'(Acts 17:23–30)

It seems from this call to 'all people everywhere' to repent, that God holds people culpable, even if they have never heard the gospel. There are essential truths about God revealed in nature, both in its external ordering and provision, and also in our internal natures. We are clearly mysteriously and wonderfully different from inanimate objects – which people call gods. Big mistake! The clues are there, says Paul.

Perhaps Paul was thinking here about their capacity to reflect and understand, their rationality and ability to recognise order in the created world, or their appreciation of art and beauty. But another feature which should certainly have alerted them was their moral awareness.

> For when the Gentiles, who do not have the law, by nature do what the law requires ... They show that the work of the law is written on their hearts, while their conscience also bears witness, and their conflicting thoughts accuse or even excuse them...when ... God judges the secrets of men by Christ Jesus. (Romans 2:14–16)

Everyone knows there are differences between right and wrong. We all experience guilt. Human beings were not left in total ignorance until they have the gospel proclaimed to them. In their consciences, they have something substantial to work on. This should stir their souls and cause them to seek after God.

The honest seeker

Paul's reference to seeking is surely significant. God's revelation in nature, as in Scripture, is clear, if subtle. It is never 'in your face'. Jesus himself spoke in parables which could be taken at face value or provoke deep questioning. He spoke of those who have eyes to see and ears to hear, implying that many would see and hear but not understand. He told people to be careful how they listen.(Luke 8:9,10,18)

He seemed particularly reticent about his own identity, commanding people in the early part of his ministry not to tell others. His teaching method was to provoke interest and draw people in, allowing others the freedom to walk away. The evidence from nature has a similar ambiguity. We can superficially say, 'How awesome!' but fail to see its implications.

The evidence of history

Again, Scripture is explicit about the importance of historical evidence. Luke starts his gospel with an emphatic claim to be providing reliable historical details. Having followed the story closely, drawing on earlier narratives and eyewitness reports, he sets out to write an orderly account, so that Theophilus might have certainty about the things he had been told (Luke 1:1–4).

When Paul spells out the historical details of his conversion and of his subsequent briefing by Peter and James, he puts himself on oath for his statements (Galatians 1:20). Swearing an oath is a solemn business for anyone, particularly for someone who believes that God will hold him to account. In 1 Corinthians 15 he lists the eyewitnesses of the resurrection and goes on to say that if this historical event is untrue, not only is their preaching in vain but they have misrepresented God, 'because we testified about God that he raised Christ, whom he did not raise' (1 Corinthians 15:14,15). In fact, this whole passage is a well-argued case, appealing to the rationality of those who might doubt it.

Matthew records that Christ taught that we should love God

with all our minds, as well as our hearts and souls (Matthew 22:37). John says that Thomas was invited by Jesus to personally test the evidence and refers to Christ's miracles as evidential 'signs' so that his disciples might believe that he is the Christ (John 20:27–31). Luke says that Jesus, after his suffering, showed himself to his apostles and 'gave many convincing proofs that he was alive' (Acts 1:3). Jesus, however, warned in the story of Dives and Lazarus, that even that truth can be ignored (though not safely ignored) by those who wish to ignore it (Luke 16:31).

The argument the apostles presented, then, was a linear one from historical events to the Lordship of Christ, and not a circular argument requiring a prior commitment to belief in an authoritative Scripture. As Martin Kahler has put it, 'We do not believe in Christ because we believe in the Bible; we believe in the Bible because we believe in Christ.'[42] It is easier, of course, just to quote a book, as every fundamentalist knows, but it invites people to put their faith in a book not a person.

How far does it go?

How, then, does natural theology work? It appeals to human nature and our capacity for rational thought and reflection, which marks us out from the rest of the animal kingdom. It is fundamental to our nature to ask questions – and life poses many of them. Certainly, some people take life for granted and ask no deeper questions about it. And if I understand Paul's letter to the Romans correctly, that refusal to ask the deeper questions is a moral choice for which people will be held responsible. The lazy, the wicked, the pleasure-seekers, the arrogant and the ungrateful will be held to account for ignoring God, because God has made himself known through what he has made.

But does natural theology leave us with a remote, deist God

who is detached and disinterested in the creation he has set in motion? The great mysteries of life provide a challenge, and both Paul and Jesus encourage the honest seeker to draw close to God. In the Sermon on the Mount, Jesus said, 'Ask and it will be given to you; seek and you will find; knock and the door will be opened to you. For everyone who asks receives; the one who seeks finds; and to the one who knocks, it will be opened' (Matthew 7:7,8).

This challenge to ask, seek and knock is given to everyone by the very fact of their existence and the realities of the world around them, which cry out for explanation. These realities bring us to an awareness of our Creator and raise questions for us as to how we should live.

'Asking' and 'seeking' speak both to our relationship to God and to our attitude towards the world around us. Knocking implies active engagement in exploring the world. At the simplest level, this could mean behaviour like the Bereans' who 'were of more noble character than the Thessalonians, for they ... examined the Scriptures every day to see if what Paul said was true'(Acts 17:11NIV). At the most technical level, it may mean building a Large Hadron Collider to explore particle physics! Augustine's great realisation, born out in Christian experience down the centuries, was that our hearts are restless, until they find their rest in God.

Preparatory work

So the world tells us about God, but on its own, it only tells us so much. Its existence speaks of the need for a transcendent Creator. Its finite character, seen both through the expansion of the universe from a singularity in the past and the second law of thermodynamics telling us that it is slowly running down, speaks of its beginning at a point in time and its predictable end.

The remarkable fine-tuning of the universe speaks strongly of an intelligent designer, and the moral awareness that is provoked by our choices tells us that our deeds matter. The beauty of the world, our deep search for love and our need for a sense of purpose testify to the intentionality of it all, and convince us that this is no random, chance, impersonal existence. Natural theology is disturbing and preparatory, teaching us fundamental truths about God, who then discloses himself in Christ to those who honestly seek him.

The Great Intender?

So who is this creator, designer, intender, lover and moral force, who presses his existence upon us? We might begin to explore all the religious ideas the world has ever produced and see if any of them are coherent, credible and satisfying. But it doesn't take long to discover that Christ is in a league of his own. There is no comparable figure in all recorded history.

And yet Christ himself draws us on. He speaks in parables, he strips us of our illusions, he throws us back on ourselves and confronts us with our own duplicity and wickedness. Jesus described himself as the Son of Man, a deliberately ambiguous title. Like a somewhat familiar stranger at a party, the guests struggle to identify him. This 'Son of Man came to seek and to save the lost'. He stills a storm, raising the question, 'Who then is this, that even the wind and the sea obey him?'(Mark 4:41). He claims authority to forgive sins against God and gives evidence of it by healing a paralysed man. He says he is the Lord of God's Sabbath, when the Jews understood that the Sabbath belonged to God (Ezekiel 20:12). He predicts that the Son of Man must suffer many things and be rejected. Then on the cross, he enters the depths of human suffering brought on by human wickedness, and offers his life in exchange for ours – for 'the Son of Man did not come to be served, but to serve, and to give his life as a ransom for many' (Matthew 20:28). Here, at last, in the crucified Christ we see the human face of God, his compassion revealed to all who honestly and humbly seek the truth. And then he bursts from the tomb in vindication and glorious triumph.

Inference to the best explanation

So natural theology can take us a very long way. It points us to the fundamental realities of our existence and provides a cumulative argument for God, while exposing the vacuum at the heart of human experience if there is no God – the nihilism of a world without meaning or value. Nature points to the balance of probabilities and an inference to the best explanation. Paul wrote that it is because of our wickedness that we suppress these truths that God has so clearly revealed to us.

The world we can observe should turn us all into seekers, and if Jesus is to be trusted, the honest seeker will always find. Even then, such a transforming encounter with Christ will not demolish all our doubts. Faith and doubt then go hand in hand. New doubts and new certainties progress together. We live by faith (trust), not by final certainty, but we have here the very best account for our extraordinary existence.

We have received an entirely credible invitation to the Great Banquet in the kingdom of God. We have good grounds for believing it. We 'dress' for the occasion by reforming our behaviour (*repentance*). We set out on the journey in anticipation, not with final certainty, but with a real hope and confident trust (*faith*). For only when we arrive at our destination will we finally be sure. As Paul wrote, 'Now I know in part; then I shall know fully, even as I have been fully known' (1 Corinthians 13:12).

The final step

November 2013 saw the fiftieth anniversary of the death of C.S.Lewis, whose personal search is well documented. The major step forward for him after years of intellectual struggle was the realisation that God must actually exist.

His step from atheism to theism was a huge stride, but the step to then acknowledge that God has revealed himself in Christ was but a short shuffle. Around his memorial stone in Poets' Corner in Westminster Abbey is his famous observation: 'I believe in Christianity as I believe that the sun has risen; not only because I see it but because by it I see everything else.'

When a person cries out to God, God makes himself known. Or as the writer of Hebrews put it, 'whoever would draw near to God must believe that he exists and that he rewards those who seek him' (Hebrews 11:6).From the dawn of time, it was ever thus.

CHAPTER 9
LAYING FIRM FOUNDATIONS

———•———

A letter in a Christian magazine recently said that in evangelism, argument should be avoided at all times. Really? People certainly don't like arguments. They divide people and they commonly lead to aggravation, drawing the very worst out of us.

Or is that a quarrel? What then is the difference between an argument and a quarrel? What is the essence of 'an argument'? Does it depend on whether it gets heated? Some people's arguments finish up as a quarrel, but that is not essential to what an argument is. It isn't an exercise in brow-beating or shouting louder, neither is it an insult to the person you are disagreeing with.

The nature of Truth

Jesus said, 'for this reason I was born, and for this I came into the world, to testify to the truth. Everyone on the side of truth listens to me' (John 18:37NIV), which led Pilate to respond with the crucial question, 'What is truth?' Dictionary definitions of 'truth' include: 'the actual state of a matter, conformity with reality, a verifiable or indisputable fact, proposition or principle'.

So truth corresponds with reality. Truth is 'what is' – and if it isn't, it isn't! Jesus said of himself, 'I am the way, the truth and the life' (John 14:6). Many people are frightened of the truth but the Christian knows that we should never be afraid of it; it is always on our side. We may not always be confident as to what the truth is in any particular matter, but we are committed to following the truth wherever it leads us. This commitment to truth has enormous implications for personal integrity, not least for what we say. We must not play fast and loose with the truth, or decorate our promises with oaths to make them sound more reliable. As Jesus put it, 'Let what you say be simply "Yes" or "No"; anything more than this comes from evil.' (Matthew 5:37).

So, if a professor is actually tired after giving a lecture, that is a truth. Wherever you are in the universe, it would still be true that this professor is now tired. There may be no one else who is feeling tired (certainly not the students who slept through the lecture), but it would still be true that the professor is tired. That is a universal truth. It remains true whether you know it or not, or whether you receive this information in Antarctica or on the moon. It is an absolute truth, not a relative truth.

Tiredness is, of course, a relative phenomenon, and the professor may be relatively more tired now than he was an hour ago and he may be more tired still by tonight, but to say that he is tired, as such, is not a relative statement. Even though he is the only one experiencing it, it is absolutely true that he is relatively tired. (I am avoiding considering the scenario of someone who says he is feeling tired when he is not. And we have all met them. They are another problem altogether!)

Some people would have us believe that 'all truth is relative'.

They claim that what is true for you isn't necessarily true for me. I have my truth and you have yours. If that were the case, the professor might be tired for you but not for me! So the statement has no objective meaning.

If it is true that 'all truth is relative', then it must be untrue, because being an absolute statement about truth, it contradicts itself. It implies that this truth anyway is not relative but absolute. Furthermore, if all truth is relative, true knowledge, including all history, science and engineering, becomes impossible. So you should never trust a bridge that has been built by a relativist. His truth may not be yours! It was to counteract this relativist view of truth which led Francis Schaeffer to resort to using the phrase 'true truth' to distinguish absolute truths from relative truths.

Logic

Fundamental to logic is the law of non-contradiction. Nothing can both be and not be. There is an either/or nature to reality, expressed in the little phrase, 'A is not Non-A'. One of the laws of logic is 'the law of the excluded middle'. Truth presents either/ or situations. It is either one thing or another, and this is the foundation of logic. It is the foundation of all rational thinking and it affects everything that we do. We get on a bus, believing it is going to the city centre. We can check whether 'City Centre' is written on the front of the bus and we can ask the driver where he is going, but in the event, he either takes us there or he doesn't. This basic structure of logic is the foundation of science. Newton, in his great experiment on light, had shone a white light through a prism and produced a rainbow. He asked, 'Why does that happen? Is it due to the light or due to the prism?' So he then shone the rainbow onto a screen and made a hole in the screen so that light of only one colour went through. When he shone the coloured light through a second prism it came out the same colour. But when he shone the whole spectrum of colours through a second prism, they came through it as white light again. He concluded that he was observing a property of white light, not a property of prisms.

That sort of deductive process is the way we negotiate our days and is the way science works. We discover truth by reason. We observe, we draw deductions, we check what we have done, we test it, we repeat it again and again. Then we draw a conclusion – but it is always a *tentative* conclusion.

Proof

Hume observed that 'proof' only occurs in the field of mathematics. For instance, in absolutely any right-angled triangle, the square of the hypotenuse is equal to the sum of the squares of the other two sides. It is always the case. But scientific proofs are not mathematical proofs. They show the apparent *weight* of evidence; there is a 'probability' of truth written into all scientific 'proofs'. This is why so many scientific truths get thrown over or at least modified over the years as science progresses.

Necessary doubt

So outside of mathematics and pure logic, all empirical truth is provisional; there are elements of doubt in all the rational conclusions that we draw. There are lots of sources for that doubt. Sensory perception is a cause of doubt. As I get older I am constantly misreading things by mis-seeing them. My wife shouts at me from downstairs and I can't hear her. I either conclude she did not say anything, or I misunderstand what she said, and we get in a frightful muddle. In the childhood game, you can put your hand into a black bag and try to identify the objects in it and be significantly mistaken – deceived by your own sensory apparatus. There are uncertainties in what we touch, hear or see. Furthermore, our brains malfunction. Memory fails. We thought a measurement was 132 centimetres, but we remembered it as 152. Our brains can get confused, forgetful and some even go insane.

Then there is the possibility that you carry a subconscious bias into a scientific experiment, of which you are completely unaware. Years ago, working in a paediatric department, our chief was called out to visit a boarding school, where the pupils had crashed out with a mystery illness. Dormitories were full of girls who had taken to their beds, apparently very unwell. He examined many of them but was completely baffled. He did not know what to make of it. So he brought the first case and the most severely affected girl into hospital that night. I was the duty doctor, and he asked me to sort it out. I worked late into the night but I could not pick up any clues as to what was wrong with them.

The next day, I was packed off to the school to take lots of blood tests and carry out other investigations. The eventual answer was that there wasn't an epidemic at all. There were several completely different and unrelated illnesses going on. Of the two girls brought into hospital, one had an irritable bowel syndrome, the other had an unusual gynaecological problem. Another girl had a streptococcal throat infection, a fourth had rubella and a fifth had glandular fever. Others were anxious that an epidemic was taking place and went down with tension headaches! The school nurse concluded wrongly that the school was being overwhelmed by a single infection. Having formed that view, she easily misled the visiting physician. It took some time to unravel it all.[43] You can carry unacknowledged prejudiced ideas and mistaken assumptions into scientific research, which colour everything.

Then, of course, wickedness can intervene, where people deliberately enter false data to achieve their desired ends. Some do it to get their research published to boost their reputation and income. You cannot always be confident about the honesty, integrity or accuracy of any human operators.

Furthermore, our understanding is limited. Sir Martin Rees, the Astronomer Royal and former president of the Royal Society, feels that the human mind may never be able to get round the difficulties of trying to unify quantum physics with Newtonian physics. This evidently creates conceptual and mathematical problems at an extreme level and he thinks we may have to live with the fact that it is irresolvable by human intelligence.

We also have limited knowledge. Stephen Hawking has made the point that trying to understand the origins of the universe may be impossible for us because we are inside the system we are trying to understand. We could only get a comprehensive understanding if we had an outside view of the system and were able to see it in its totality, including what happened at the beginning.

There is a great deal to life that we cannot understand. Just recently, salmon migration has been explained by magnetic forces, which guide them over vast distances and bring them back to the place where they were spawned. Who would have thought it was due to magnetism?

We cannot see the past or the future: we have some limited artefacts from the past but know nothing about the future – we can only guess or dream it. We can, of course, try to shape it, but we live only in the present, but that itself is but a fleeting moment. Ironically that moment which I experience in my brain as being 'now' is itself already in the past by the time I realise it. It takes time for sensations to reach the brain and for the brain to register what is going on. So all we have is actually in the past and those records, including our memories, are all we can draw upon.

A humble view of truth

So we need to have a humble view of truth. This applies to the two books of truth which Augustine and Francis Bacon wrote about – the book of nature and the book of Scripture. Studying the book of nature by science is difficult, costly and limited. For instance, to take particle physics significantly beyond the capacity of the Large Hadron Collider would need a research tool so much bigger that the size would be unimaginable, and the cost unthinkable.

But understanding Scripture is not without its difficulties, either. Christians do not believe the Bible was dictated by God. Rather, God spoke through individuals who lived at points in space-time history. So we have a 'hermeneutic' problem in trying first to understand what it originally meant in the mind of the author, and what he hoped his original readers would understand in their historic context. Only then can we go on to ask what this text means for us today. What was the situation in Corinth, for example, when Paul wrote to them? We only know a limited amount about it, so we may well misunderstand some crucial issues.

Sometimes, we in the present might understand something better than they did in the past. Did the Philistines understand that the pituitary tumour, far and away the most likely cause of Goliath's gigantism, was also liable to cause him visual field defects, making him vulnerable by being unable to see fully? He may not have seen David properly, let alone the stone expelled from his sling!

If something is true in science, or true in history or theology, these matters are true. And there is a unity in truth. Truth does not contradict itself, though it may appear to, as with quantum and Newtonian physics. And it may be impossible for us to unify certain apparent truths. Whether or not we can demonstrate what is actually true, the fact remains that what is actually true is ultimately consistent with whatever else is true, wherever it is to be found. If it is true, it is true. As Francis Bacon, who became known as the Father of Experimental Science, put it:' It is a pleasure to stand up on the shore and see ships tossed upon the sea; a pleasure to stand in the window of a castle...and see the adventures below: but no pleasure is comparable to the standing upon the vantage ground of truth.'[44]

So what then is an argument?

An argument is the way we tease out what is true and distinguish it from falsehood. This is done logically in our minds, when we decide 'this' is not 'that'; A is not non-A. We make deductions and discuss them with others. The simplest logical deduction would be that if A=B and B=C, then A=C.

That is an argument – and a compelling one! The Greek mathematician Euclid, in around 300BC, expressed this as the first of his 'five common notions'. Things that are equal to the same thing are equal to each other. If you think your conclusion is mistaken, that A cannot equal C, you have to call into question one of the premises from which your conclusion was drawn. You are effectively saying either that A does not equal B, or that B does not equal C. One must be wrong (and it is possible that both are wrong). This, at its simplest, is how we do our reasoning.

Probabilities

So, logical deductions challenge the strength of the premises. What evidence is there for premise A=B? Or for premise B=C? In practice, you finish up asking, 'Are they both more likely to be true or untrue?' Which has the greater *probability*? As we can't be 100 per cent confident of any truth outside of mathematics and logic, we must act always on what is *probably* true, and this applies to all of science and all of faith.

At this moment in time, my stomach feels ready for lunch and I also heard the tap being turned on in the kitchen. On those two premises, I could conclude that it is time to go downstairs. However, I have been disappointed in the past. While my stomach is a fairly reliable indicator of lunchtime, I have found that my wife does do other things in the kitchen: she could be about to wash the floor. I will therefore carry on typing a little longer until some other signal is given, perhaps the smell of cooking or a call from the cook. (Even then I have been disappointed, particularly if my daughter phones just when her mother is about to serve the food. It often happens! So is it lunchtime or not? It can be very difficult to know.) So we have to balance probabilities. Is it more probable that it is true or untrue? We take action accordingly. (As for me, I am going to give it another five minutes before going downstairs!)

Knowledge?

What, then, is knowledge? Some say knowledge is true belief, but I think it is better to say that it is warranted true belief. We have to be clear what a given proposition is and what the grounds are for believing it, especially when considering empirical truth-claims. For example, we might meet someone who is convinced the moon is made of cheese. They may believe it passionately, but why should we believe it without good evidence? (This, it seems to me, is the fundamental flaw in Barthian theology, which I discussed earlier.)

So we have to check our assumptions and our conclusions to see if they are warranted. A lot of the things we think we know are, in fact, mistaken. But in terms of a working definition of what knowledge is, it is a belief that you have good grounds – a warrant – to think it is true, even if you cannot ultimately prove it. In other words, it is more probably true than untrue and you base future activity upon that belief.

Argument, within our own minds or with other people, is the way we sort out what we can 'know' and trust to be true, over against what is untrue and untrustworthy.

Certainly, those who can't argue properly frequently quarrel, but that is a problem of temperament and manners. It isn't essential to get hot under the collar when you make a logical deduction. That usually implies that the truth of the issue in dispute is somewhat threatening to us. We don't like its implications. Such emotions do nothing to undermine the validity of the fact that rational argument is the essential process in the human quest for truth.

CHAPTER 10
PROPOSITIONS IN A POSTMODERN CULTURE

———•———

In 2007, I chaired a lecture for students in Oxford. The subject was the reasons for belief in God. After the lecture, a distinguished-looking elderly man took me aside and berated me for thinking that 'propositional evangelism' could work nowadays in sophisticated Oxford. Professorial in appearance, he evidently thought the lecture was worse than a waste of time. He felt it was counterproductive and would drive thinking people away from God.

I was a bit taken aback that he felt so negatively about an excellent lecture given, of all people, by the renowned philosopher and theologian William Lane Craig. I suspect this man wasn't a philosopher, scientist, engineer or a mathematician. He may have been a social scientist, an historian or an artist, but almost certainly he was a postmodernist. Propositional evangelism fell into disrepute since the 1960s with the rise of postmodernism, which is shot through with relative thinking. Religion is now seen to be a subjective affair and should be communicated by 'telling your personal story', not presenting 'propositional truth' statements.

Relativists hold that 'Man is the measure of all things' and that truth lies in the eye of the beholder. Truth is what you perceive it to be and it is not appropriate to talk about truth as being 'out there' and the same for everyone. Similarly, ethical relativists believe there are no objective, morally binding principles. Of course, different observers will have different perspectives and understand truth in the different contexts of their own lives. But that does not imply there is no truth out there with universal implications.

Postmodernism is a sceptical movement which sees truth as being socially constructed. It began as a response to art, architecture and then music, before impacting on philosophy. It is complex and difficult to understand, and its roots are hotly disputed, not least because of the diversity of viewpoints among postmodern writers. But the net effect challenges the whole system of values in the Western world. Truth, they claim, is to be understood internally. It comprises a whole perspective on reality and generally opposes 'realism'. It rejects the idea that our 'knowledge' can be an accurate representation of reality. The causes of events are not at all obvious and many unidentified factors contribute to what we observe.

A major theme in all this is the tension between subjective experience and objective reality. People caught up in this cultural movement are likely to recoil from any discussion of things being true in an absolute sense. For them, Christianity is a lived-out experience, not a set of doctrines, and as a result it is 'caught not taught'. Faith is communicated by warm feelings of love and friendship, rather than cold, detached statements about truth. Factual information and logical deductions on this basis change no one. Religions exist in a marketplace of ideas, and who is to say that one idea is true and another not? In this cultural climate, the only effective evangelism is relational, based on personal narrative, where anyone's views are as valid as everyone else's.

In this context, Francis of Assisi became the patron saint of relational evangelism with the oft-quoted saying, 'Preach the gospel at all times; and if necessary, use words.' There is apparently no good evidence that he ever said that – but it captures the postmodern mood succinctly.

So what is this 'propositional evangelism' that drives postmodernists to distraction? Propositions are assertions/claims that something or other is true – that it accords with reality, is non-contradictory and is absolutely and universally true. Christian faith is full of such propositions – that God exists, that he created the universe, designed its natural laws, spoke through certain people and that he has revealed himself uniquely in Christ in a certain geographic location at a given point in history. He fulfilled ancient prophecies, was raised from the dead and will one day call us all to account. These are all propositions – which may or may not be true. If they are true, they are true for everyone, including postmodern academics, not just for those who think they are true.

The apostles proclaimed these things, but they did not just go out and tell the gospel story. They argued and persuaded the world that these propositions are actually, physically and historically true. As a result of their preaching, people became convinced that the central proposition– that the resurrection was a space-time historical event– was actually true.

But postmodernists find that very difficult to hear. They want to add that little phrase, 'for me' at the end. 'The resurrection may be true for me but not necessarily for anyone else.' The implication is that Christians should stop proclaiming the resurrection as something that is true or false in objective terms. We can offer it as a subjective experience or a way of looking at faith, as long as we leave everyone to come to their own faith experience, which will be different for everyone, and not insist that 'true truths' are involved.

Needless to say, the apostle Paul would have had great difficulty with that! He taught that 'if Christ is not been raised, then our preaching is in vain and your faith is in vain. We are even found to be misrepresenting God, because we testified about God that he raised Christ, whom he did not raise if it is true that the dead are not raised... And if Christ has not been raised, your faith is futile and you are still in your sins. Then... we are of all people most to be pitied' (1 Corinthians 15:14–19).

In other words, Paul was resolute in antithetical thinking (A is not non-A). Here is the logic of 'the excluded middle'. The truth is either one or the other. It is a black or white matter. It cannot be both true and untrue, and there is no room here for shades of grey. Neither can it be true for some people and not true for others. As Professor Sir Norman Anderson wrote concerning the resurrection:

If it is true, it is the supreme fact of history, and to fail to adjust one's life to its implications means irreparable loss. If it is not true...then the whole of Christianity is a fraud, foisted on the world by a company of consummate liars, or at best, deluded simpletons.[45]

Anderson was a lawyer, and lawyers look for a verdict – guilty or not guilty. Everyone waits with bated breath as the jury delivers their verdict. If there is not sufficient evidence to convict, the prisoner is found 'Not guilty' and the judge sets him free. He does not say he is guilty in the eyes of some but not of others, and so sentence him to five years of alternate months in prison, to do justice to both opposing viewpoints.

Surgeons also have real difficulties over the 'excluded middle' option. They wait impatiently while the physicians fluff around. Their only question is, 'Do we cut it off or not?' There is no middle ground. If it is a cancer, they will not cure the patient by only taking it half off. When it comes to amputation, it is all or nothing.

Aeronautical engineers have to face up to the excluded middle. The plane they make will either fly or not. No one is remotely interested in it taking off and getting 80 per cent of the way there before plunging into the sea. Death itself has an absolute nature about it. One in one die, however much we wished that was untrue. Postmodernists say it is arrogant to know you are right. It may seem like that, but it is also arrogant and enormously foolish to say it doesn't matter!

If we apply the dictum attributed to St Francis to Jesus, we find that Jesus demonstrated the love of God in action by caring for people. But he also used words to teach compassion and was himself described as the Logos – the Word made flesh. Deeds alone were not enough for him. They had to be interpreted using language. He proclaimed the kingdom of God in speech and action – and that is the balance that we have to find.

However, if you envisage propositional evangelism as a confrontational exercise, where Christians tell others in an authoritative way what they feel people need to hear, we have misunderstood both the gospel and the culture we are in.

Consider the story of Philip evangelising the Ethiopian eunuch (Acts 8:26–39). He didn't stop his chariot and confront him with truth he wasn't ready to hear. He asked the Ethiopian whether he understood what he was reading and then, after being explicitly invited on board, sat alongside him shoulder to shoulder as they journeyed together, helping him to explore the truth that lay before – and outside – them both. The dynamics of this are really important. Philip started at the place where the Ethiopian was, on a chariot reading Isaiah chapter 53. We need to think where postmodernists are sitting, if we realistically hope to gain a hearing.

Postmodern secularists are caught up in a culture which hinders them from considering objective truths. And Christian people, living in the same world, are also liable to be profoundly affected by it. So when they endeavour to do evangelism, they usually major on anecdotes, tell their own personal story, look for felt needs in the person they are talking to, and emphasise subjective experiences. Modernist Christians are liable to be more confrontational and less personal; they will major on objective facts and come away consoling themselves that they have done their duty and told the unbeliever what he needs to hear!

A survey in 1991 apparently showed that 72 per cent of Americans aged eighteen to twenty-five believed 'there is no such thing as absolute truth'. It would be interesting to know how they would answer that question today. My 'feeling' (a word I use cautiously in the circumstances) is that those numbers may have dropped. I rarely hear people now arguing that all truth is relative. The tide may be turning and there are good reasons why it should. Science, engineering and justice would be impossible in postmodern terms! Relativism is a no-brainer for car drivers, or for people who cross roads or take medicines. No one thinks when picking up an umbrella that it might rain 'just for me'. It is also a no-brainer for anyone who understands that the relativist's claim 'there is no such thing as absolute truth' is itself an absolute truth claim. Relativism cannot even be stated, let alone lived by consistently.

Nonetheless, I suspect many young people have bought into relativism at some level, including the level of religious ideas. They are less dogmatic, less logical, but more experience-centred and more tolerant of divergent opinions than older generations. They think in terms of truth being 'true for me' and hold to the idea that we somehow create our own truth.

Thirty years ago, when relativism was at its height, I did an Eastertide radio debate with the president of the British National Secular Society. I was invited to speak first and Barbara Smoker then followed by saying that she welcomed the fact that she and I were both in agreement that the resurrection either happened or it didn't. The story was either true or false. It couldn't be true for some but not true for others.

I was delighted. I thought we had started in the right place and had established antithetical thinking (A≠non-A) at the outset. On that basis, I happily put forward my arguments. She was robustly hostile to Christ, and ridiculed the 'wicked' idea of judgement. This also is an either/or matter, so I was happy to maintain the absolute nature of the possibilities. I gave my closing remarks and finally she gave hers: 'Well, I am sorry for you, Dr May, that you believe in the Judgement. But it won't happen to me, because I don't believe in it!'

In my mind, I heard my old Aussie mentor, Chappo, exclaiming, 'Say something relevant!' Believing it doesn't make it true or untrue. That has to be decided on other grounds. The shocker for me was that having established antithetical thinking at the outset, and maintained it throughout the debate, it should be thrown on the rubbish pile in her closing statement.

But that is what happens with relativism. We cannot live

consistently with it because our lives are caught up in objective reality. So people slide in and out of relativism, making antithetical thought difficult to maintain.

Needless to say, a whole package of values has been ushered in by this way of thinking. To try to paint a word picture here, consider these lists. Postmodernists *tend to dislike* conformity, status, formality, qualifications, expertise, certainties, history, deference, tradition, respectability, conservatism, hierarchy, institutions, unity, power structures, boundaries, difficulties, universals, exclusivity, purpose, control, tidiness, logic, rationality, theorising, planning, elitism, dogma, creeds, professionalism, and God the Father.

Instead, they *tend to prefer* individualism, egalitarianism, freedom, gifting, hospitality, choice, experiences, tolerance, novelty, opinions, immediacy, honesty, informality, sincerity, alternative therapies, transience, fragmentation, collage, decentralisation, risk-taking, localism, diversity, spontaneity, play, casual dress, pick & mix, mysticism, social action, short-termism, community, radicalism, narrative, lay leadership, and the Holy Spirit. In a postmodern culture the only certainty is uncertainty, and the ultimate virtue is tolerance.

It is evident from this that postmodernism is far-reaching. These attitudes are 'breathed in' from the surrounding culture, and they affect almost everything, not least the media and current education policies.

Yesterday, I spoke to a doctor who is studying in London to be a trainer of family doctors. He feels that the whole of his course is shot through with postmodernism. For instance, the focus is entirely on student-centred learning. It has nothing to do with a hierarchical analysis of what a good doctor would need to know, but has everything to do with what his own felt needs are. The trainee decides. The course is entirely personal and subjective, whether in developing his consultation skills, in the reading he pursues, the ethics he lives by and the way he evaluates his own work.

Now, the doctors on the course were each asked to research and deliver a presentation. Inevitably in such an atmosphere, the subject matter was not dictated by the course 'directors' (surely they should have been called 'conveners'?) but the trainees could choose whatever they felt was really important to them from what they had been learning.

So this particular doctor decided to present his concerns about the postmodernism that was dominating his course. A course director attended his presentation. The doctor challenged his audience about the objective nature of truth and reality. He exposed some of the difficulties with 'modernism' before embarking on the problems of postmodernism, and its 'relative' take on reality. I would love to have been a fly on the wall!

Eventually, the course director stood up and announced that he didn't believe in reality, and added, 'Furthermore, I don't want reality' and then stormed out of the room. (I wanted to know if he *really* did storm out or whether his departure was his own subjective illusion. However, if he slammed the door it should have been heard by everyone!)

Society is going through rapid change and the church is necessarily caught up in this shifting culture. Not everything in the old, 'modern' worldview is valuable. There are major problems in our confidences about truth and scientific 'proof'. Neither is everything in the postmodern world to be dismissed. These values need sifting by a 'critical realism'. We need to hold on to what was good from the past and embrace what is good in these new perspectives.

It follows from all this that if young postmodern people are to hear the truths of the gospel, we need to take these cultural issues very seriously. We should develop relationships with the people we want to address and should look for informal contexts. We must avoid talking down at them and always engage in careful dialogue. Many of our difficulties in communication are due to our different understandings of the same words, not least what we mean by 'truth'! We also need to understand their viewpoints, and make good use of 'story' in explaining our points, including our personal stories. We *must* practise hospitality (not an optional extra, according to Paul in Romans 12:13) and follow Christ's example of making good use of mealtimes, as well as other acts of kindness and friendship. We should also avoid heavy-handed dogmatism and condescending judgementalism.

As we engage in dialogue, we must be on our guard for relative thinking. One of the commonest ways we walk into it is by saying, 'I believe...' The moment we do that we are encouraging an exchange of all sorts of equally 'valuable' ideas that people may believe. And we don't need to use the 'B' word! What we 'believe' is actually irrelevant. What matters is what is actually true. So it is much better to say, 'Jesus taught this... the apostle Paul wrote that... the Gospel writers claimed...' This promptly establishes our thinking outside of subjectivism and places the burden on the history and credibility of the source you quote. True, you may then have to defend the historicity of the New Testament documents, but then you should learn how to give reasons for the hope you have that they are reliable and authentic. The documents are fundamental to the Christian case.

Many people resort to 'I believe...' statements because they prefer to avoid saying 'The Bible says...' as they would then end up having to defend the most difficult Bible passages. The person might reply, 'So you believe the Bible, do you? What about Noah's ark, Jonah and the whale, the genocide of the Canaanites, the six days of creation...' All this and more, when you were trying to have a conversation about the person of Christ! The phrases 'I believe' and 'The Bible says...' are both unnecessary and may seriously distract you from your purpose.

In conclusion, we need to come to terms with the cultural revolution that is going on around us. All viewpoints and conversations are being influenced and shaped by postmodernism, but more so in the Arts than in the Sciences. If we don't recognise that and fail to take deliberate steps to engage with the postmodern context, we will find a very much smaller pool of people who are interested in hearing what we have to say.

CHAPTER 11
INTUITION AND KNOWING

There is clearly more to the process of knowing than observation and logical deduction. Sometimes we have deep convictions that something is true and we may be hard put to justify it. These realisations can come in a flash. We may have been puzzled by appearances, circumstances or events over a long period, but suddenly it all falls into place. Like the two at supper in Emmaus, truth suddenly dawns (Luke 24:31).

Doctors commonly have this experience when confronted by an ill patient. We have a deep insight that something here is seriously wrong but we can't make sense of the particulars. The symptoms don't tally with our observations. We sense that the patient is ill and needs to be admitted to hospital urgently, but the difficulty comes when you try to explain your reasons on the phone to the hospital doctor on duty. He wants hard data before responding to your subjective whim.

In my first year as a trainee general practitioner, I had a very disconcerting on-call, duty weekend. I reported back to my trainer on Monday morning about the difficulties I had experienced. I felt I had lost my clinical judgement. Over the weekend, I had admitted seven people to hospital. I might normally have expected to admit one or two – but seven? And they all struck me as being so ill – yet I couldn't make a confident diagnosis on any of them. My wise trainer said, 'Let's discuss them at the end of the week, when you have heard back from the hospital.'

It was quite a shock to me to learn that three of the seven had died in hospital within a few hours. Another had severe pneumonia and was responding slowly to antibiotics. All my 'gut feelings' had been right, though I could not make sense of any of them at the time. There had not been a malingerer among them.

Here is a different example. A stranger came to the front door. He was doing a survey and asked if he could interview me. I did not recognise the name of the firm he worked for, but I invited him in. I made him a coffee and he fired questions at me for half an hour. My wife returned home just as I was showing him out.

'Who was that?' she asked.

'I don't know. His name was John and he was conducting a survey.'

'And you let him in?' she said, shaking her head in disbelief. 'Why?'

It wasn't an easy question to answer. He was pleasant. He greeted me with a smile. He looked at me straight in the eyes – and, oh yes, he laughed at a joke I made. (She did not think any of those were valid reasons for inviting him in!)

An awful lot of evaluations we make about people, situations, conditions and issues are made in a split second – and we learn to trust our judgements. While the formal processes of reasoning and deduction, whether in science, maths, logic or philosophy, are largely attributed to activity in the left hemisphere of the brain, these short-cut, intuitive judgements are held to be more right brain activities. Women, they say, are better at it than men, but I couldn't possibly comment.

Interestingly, the 'eureka' flashes of insight and inspiration seem to be as common among scientists and mathematicians as they are among artists. The artist may describe them in inspirational terms and the religious person may consider them 'epiphanies'. The scientist may call them moments of 'realisation' after wrestling for years with a conundrum. But call them what you will, we all get them. And sometimes they even occur in our sleep and we wake up with an urgent need to write down our thoughts. Jung thought such perceptions erupt from our unconscious states.

Before we divide the world into two types of people, the deductives and the intuitives, the methodicals and the imaginatives, the dull-witted sluggards and the inspiring people with flair, we need to ask some harder questions.

Why does a doctor make immediate assessments that a patient is seriously ill, even though he cannot justify it? I suspect it works like this. There is something in the initial phone call that sounds a warning. Perhaps it is apprehension in the voice of the caller, together with a confusing story. As you enter the home, you may pick up particular 'vibrations'. It may be a smell, a sense of disorganisation, or the appearance of neglect. As soon as you see the patient, you notice, but may not remember or record, that they look pale, clammy and frightened. As they answer your questions, they are clearly not on top of the situation. Their account is muddled and incoherent.

Of course, you examine them. The chest sounds clear, the heart rate is regular if perhaps rapid, the abdomen is soft and you detect no clear signs of serious illness. But against the backdrop of those subliminal warning lights, you admit them to hospital and are not surprised to learn that they die within a few hours.

Whilst we put some of our observations into verbal thoughts, most of what we observe is grasped in an instant. The details are not separated out into conscious statements of fact. We get glimpses of things out of the corner of the eye and hear subtle sounds that may not consciously register. It may only be later that we are able to identify some of these first impressions, but many go unacknowledged. The same is true for everyone in decision-making.

The more experienced we are, the greater is our ability to pick up clues and to recognise patterns. In just four days in Barcelona, my wife and I experienced five attempts at robbery. We became highly sensitised to the levels of street crime in that wonderful city. The thieves rarely worked alone and we became alert to 'shifty' glances between people, of sudden unexpected movements, of close encounters and 'funny' situations developing in front of us.

Intuition is a learned ability and it is closely related to our imaginative ability. This is one of the reasons that young drivers have more tragic accidents than old codgers. These kids just cannot imagine what might lie around the corner. The older person has been round more corners. We get wiser as we get older and realise the implications of the risks we might be taking.

Childcare is similar. On one occasion, I was left supervising bath time for four grandchildren. 'No problem,' I thought. One little mite was in the bath, a second needed a nappy change. A third decided (why was I surprised by this?) to closely examine the disgusting contents of the said nappy, while the fourth, who could barely walk, used the opportunity to head off downstairs. There was no one around to help. A complex situation had suddenly developed in under a minute. I have not allowed that to happen again! We learn by such experiences.

How does all this relate to the way we hear the gospel? Exploring Christianity involves checking out a number of detailed, data-driven issues (the grounds for belief in God, the evidence of the New Testament documents etc.). But the issues of the gospel address the deepest mysteries of life, and therefore the mysteries in our own lives: the search for love, the quest for meaning, our sense of values, our moral responsibility. We cannot read through the Gospel accounts without these profound issues of the human 'heart' being jolted and shaken within us.

In this context, we need to consider the role of the Holy Spirit. Jesus taught that after his departure, he would send his disciples 'the Counsellor' (John 16:7,8NIV), whom he also called 'the Spirit of truth', who would be at work within them and among them (John 16:13).It was the Spirit's role to 'convict the world concerning sin and righteousness and judgment' (John 16:8). In other words, he prompts our consciences about our moral failings, demonstrates to us the beauty of goodness revealed in Christ, and the inevitability that we will be held to account for our failings, when evil is eventually overthrown.

Such realisations can hit us like a torrent. We might suddenly grasp that our assumptions have been fundamentally wrong. Not only does God exist but he stands before us in Christ. Our eyes are opened. All of a sudden, the world looks different. We can see things now that we could not see or imagine beforehand.

I realise that many people seem to come gradually into Christian belief and conviction. Such people may say that five years ago they were not Christians or remotely interested in God. Yet today, their lives are utterly caught up with the wonder of God, revealed in Christ. Don't ask them when they became Christians. They do not know! All they know is that sometime in the last five years they have become Christians.

For myself, there was a definite moment of 'epiphany'. A reductionist will try to explain this away in psychological terms and I suspect that that may all be true – but not the whole truth. There are other levels of explanation that paint a fuller picture. At 9.30p.m. on Tuesday, 17 May 1966, at the age of twenty, after listening to the preaching of a man called Dan Piatt in Duke Street Baptist Church in Richmond, I came into a momentary and profound realisation that Christianity was true. It was as though the curtain was pulled back, if just for a brief moment – but enough for me to gasp in wonder.

Why do I think this cannot be explained purely in psychological terms? Firstly, it did not happen in a vacuum. I had in the previous three years read the New Testament through carefully three times. I had become increasingly convinced of the integrity of these documents, persuaded of the centrality of the resurrection and the compelling nature of the apostolic testimony. The person of Christ was already shining as a very bright light before me.

Secondly, something else happened, and when I tell this story no one believes it. But here goes. For the previous five years, I had nurtured a strong ambition to be a doctor and in each of the previous three years I had applied for a place at medical school. The bit some people *can* believe is that I had been repeatedly unsuccessful! The unbelievable bit is that I had actually been rejected thirty-one times! It couldn't happen nowadays, but it was possible – for the very obstinate – in London in the mid-1960s. But this was to be the end of it. The rules had been changed, and anyway, parental patience had now worn out, so I had no real chance of applying again.

The night I became a Christian, I was filled with optimism

that God must have some other career plan for me, but then I remembered there was just one more medical school which I had yet to hear from. So this had to be God's call! The 'coin', as it were, had been tossed and was already spinning in the air. To everyone's surprise, I was called for interview. This was only the second medical school that actually asked to see me. So on my thirty-second application (is that a National All-comers record?), in October 1966 I was offered a place to start at medical school the following year.

Amongst the immediate effects Christian conversion had on me was an irresistible desire to read and study. Thirdly, the world around me suddenly became very interesting. Apart from the sciences, I had never worked hard at school. Now I wanted to understand history, literature, geography, politics and the humanities. I embarked on an orgy of reading. New light was being shone on everything.

I take it from the New Testament that it is the work of the Holy Spirit to enable us to see truth. Jesus said the Spirit of truth 'dwells with you and will be in you' (John 14:16, 17).

Paul wrote that people 'by their unrighteousness suppress the truth. For what can be known about God is plain to them, because God has shown it to them' (Romans 1:18,19). So there is a battle for truth going on in the human soul. God by his Spirit alerts us to the deeper realities of life's meaning and significance. We, in our wickedness, look the other way. If that is true, every non-Christian is living in tension with the realities he experiences. God points things out to us but we wilfully turn a blind eye.

In the Spanish Civil War, Madrid was surrounded by four columns of Nationalist troops. Their general, Emilio Mola, famously told a journalist in 1936 that he had a fifth column of supporters actually in Madrid itself, who would work for the overthrow of the Republicans.

Similarly, in every non-Christian we talk to, there is an inner conflict going on, between the truth illuminated by God's Spirit and its suppression by the individual who struggles to maintain his autonomy. We need to recognise that the Holy Spirit is at work, engaging with their conscience and understanding, and cooperate with him as he undermines the rebellion of their soul. Sometimes, we just need to be patient and pray.

Leighton Ford told this story. A professor in semantics from the University of California attended a series of meetings where Paul Little spoke about Christ's resurrection.

> He [the professor] was a complete relativist in his thinking. He advanced the popular idea that what we believe is true to us but not necessarily true for other people, and he used this illustration: A man may be tied on a railroad track. When a train whizzes by on the next track he dies of a heart attack for he does not know it was not on his track. He believed it was and it became true for him. Time and again we tried to show this professor the significant difference in Christianity, the fact of the resurrection. About the fourth time around, the penny dropped. Standing at the blackboard with a piece of chalk in his hand, he suddenly stopped in mid-sentence and said, 'Hum... yes, that would make a difference,' and sat down.[46]

While the search for truth can be a dogged experience of spade work as individuals turn over the issues, at other times truth suddenly dawns upon the soul. Huge realisations can be grasped in a moment. Connections between diverse ideas suddenly come together. Arguments that have been stacking up suddenly become overwhelming, while contrary arguments collapse. A detailed but confusing map suddenly gets correctly orientated. Once north is identified, everything else falls into place. Yes, there may have been careful logic and deduction going on. But yes, there are also sudden insights and flashes of understanding, which alter the entire picture.

This may be due to a sudden switch of assumptions. For instance, if God does not exist, then the New Testament miracles were clearly impossible. Certainly, Christ's healing miracles cannot be verified from this point in history, so why should they be believed? But if God exists and raised Christ from the dead, the reasons to disbelieve them are left hanging in the air. As the professor said, 'Yes, that would make a difference.'

However long people struggle with doubts and unbelief, the dawning of faith can be sudden and overwhelming. And I expect that is commonly the case. Whenever I hear a large crowd sing Charles Wesley's famous hymn 'And can it be?' it seems to gain such momentum in the fourth verse. Rarely are other hymns sung with quite such passion:

> Long my imprisoned spirit lay,
> Fast bound in sin and nature's night;
> Thine eye diffused a quickening ray –
> I woke, the dungeon flamed with light;
> My chains fell off, my heart was free,
> I rose, went forth, and followed Thee.

(Charles Wesley, 1707–78)

CHAPTER 12
DEALING WITH DOUBT

————•————

What is doubt?

Doubt is often seen to be the opposite of faith, but as such, it becomes demonised, being seen as an expression of spiritual and moral failure. This distorted view can have serious consequences. Young people, especially those brought up as Christians, are liable to lose their childhood faith if they do not feel free to check it out for themselves. They will have their own questions, shaped by their own experience and culture. They cannot expect that their parents' faith, however well-established it was, can just be passed on to them. Chappo used to major the point that there are no 'Family Tickets' into the kingdom of God. We have to come one at a time. All children have to face the issues for themselves. Doubt is not the opposite of faith so much as the opposite of confidence and conviction about God. And such doubt is not limited to religion. Outside of mathematics, the whole world of knowledge is beset with doubts. How can we know anything with certainty? Can I trust my senses? As we have considered, they are certainly not infallible.

Sometimes we dream. I dreamt very vividly the other night and woke up rather disorientated. I had been in another world, fortunately an imaginary one, but it seemed very real at the time. Whether it was due to something I ate or the fact that it was very warm, I don't know, but it was an unpleasant experience. Os Guinness in his classic book on Doubt, quotes Lao-Tze's disturbing question: 'If when I was asleep I was a man dreaming I was a butterfly, how do I know when I am awake that I am not a butterfly dreaming I am a man?'[47]

Scientific truth

After the confidence of Logical Positivism sixty years ago, the world of science has adopted a more humble approach to knowing. All scientific truths are now seen as provisional. They can all expect to be modified or overthrown in the passage of time. Sometimes our understanding takes a quantum leap forward where known 'facts' take on a totally new appearance as part of a bigger picture.

The world is a lot more mysterious than we used to think it was, and scientists themselves are much more fallible than we previously thought. They can also be less than honest in the way they publish their findings. A senior Japanese stem cell researcher committed suicide last year after one of his team tampered with the published results.

Every genuine discovery is liable to open up greater complexities. The more we learn, the more we find there is to learn. As knowledge increases, we realise that we know even less than we thought. Climbing one hill, we see the next. Every substantial answer opens up new questions, while new discoveries help us develop new technologies, which enable us to explore the world more deeply.

Faith and certainty

A common misunderstanding is that faith somehow takes over when knowledge is exhausted, but the reality is that faith assumptions underlie all our knowledge. Believing the world is real and not a dream, believing that what is detected by my senses approximates to the realities around me, and believing that my thought processes can make sense of it are all very difficult to prove. We assume, for instance, that light always travels in straight lines, when actually we know it doesn't. And we assume we are not hallucinating, when we know that those who are hallucinating are quite convinced they are not!

A major problem with our ability to know anything is that very little of our knowledge have we been able to investigate for ourselves. Nearly everything we know is taken on trust (i.e. faith) in the discoveries of other people, even in science. The scientist has to trust other scientists in his team and they must all trust the equipment they use. They then must trust their own intelligence and rationality, that they haven't overlooked something fundamental and that they have properly (if not fully) understood the issues under investigation. They also have to trust the consistency of the natural world, that objects do not spring into existence without causes, and that our observations today enable us to make accurate predictions about tomorrow.

An interesting example of the provisional nature of science arose in the vexed parliamentary debate on equal marriage. Medical scientist, Lord Winston said that the evidence that gay couples make better parents than heterosexual parents was 'incontrovertible'. It was an extraordinary thing for a scientist to say. The whole history of science cries out against him that any scientific knowledge could be considered 'incontrovertible'. He even referred to a specific researcher – he obviously had 'great faith' in her work! The government spokesman had great faith in Lord Winston and repeated his claim in her closing statement. So can the nation have faith that science has clearly documented the superior benefits of gay parenting?

The answer is 'no'. The research in question was done on very small samples of people who actually volunteered to take part. It was therefore a self-selecting group of parents who were confident enough in their parenting to subject it to rigorous enquiry. It was also one-sided, as the researchers did not seek the opinions of their children. Neither did they compare their findings with the parenting of stable, heterosexual marriages. Subsequent research on a very much larger number of randomly selected (but now adult) children, who were representative of the population at large, and using a proper control group for comparison, showed the opposite to be the case.[48] So a heated public debate continues. So-called scientific knowledge is not certain knowledge. It is never final and complete. It is sometimes biased, is always provisional and likely to be challenged, modified or overthrown by subsequent discoveries. As Paul put it, 'For now we know in part' (1 Corinthians 13:12). That is true for all human knowledge.

Simple truth

Consider a simple matter of an invitation to a fancy dress party, which you gladly accept. You note the date and the time on the invitation. But then you discover that the invitation is for a Saturday but the given date is actually a Sunday. We have all made such mistakes. You phone for clarification. While you were on the phone, you check the venue details. In due course you set out – but is it in knowledge or in faith? You won't know until you arrive whether the time, date and venue are actually correct. Also it required further faith on your part as you thought about what to wear, and more faith again was required when you paid for the hire of your fabulous chicken outfit with flapping wings. (You also trust, of course, that no one else will have thought of that!) It was going to be such fun – until you arrive at the venue to be told that the invitation said evening dress not fancy dress. Faith in our memories is deeply bound up in all our knowing.

So knowing doesn't exist without faith, but faith is not a matter of plucking ideas out of thin air, aided only by a vivid imagination. Christian faith, anyway, is deeply rooted in objective facts – about the nature of the universe in general, humankind in particular, and specific historical data about Christ.

Putting truth into action

I recently visited the Normandy beaches, which seventy years ago were the scene of the greatest military invasion in human history. General Dwight D. Eisenhower had to make probably the biggest decision any mortal has ever had to face. I break into a cold sweat just thinking about it. This vast armada, assembled over the previous two years with its own huge, untested, portable 'home-made' harbour (code named 'Mulberry') was ready to sail on 5 June 1944. The weather forecast was so bad he had to delay the invasion by twenty-four hours. That was the easy decision!

The next day saw only a partial improvement. The success of their plans depended on a full moon and a mid-rising tide at the break of dawn. This was the last chance to meet these three criteria for about a month. Eisenhower was asked to make the decision. After a prolonged silence, he turned to General Montgomery. 'What would you do?' Monty, with less than ringing conviction, replied, 'I think I would go.'

Their doubts concerned what US secretary of defence, Donald Rumsfeld famously called 'the unknowns'. Concerning the invasion of Iraq, he said, 'There are known knowns. There are things we know we know. We also know there are known unknowns; that is to say we know there are some things that we do not know. But there are also unknown unknowns – the ones we don't know we don't know.'[49]

For the invasion of Normandy, these doubts focused around the uncertainties of the weather. Would the Mulberry harbour and the many small craft survive the crossing, and allow the successful landing of the largest invasion force ever assembled? And what would be the unforeseen consequences of a further delay? Would the Nazis learn about the Normandy plan, removing the key element of surprise? It was arguably the toughest decision that anyone has ever had to make!

Looked at in this way, it becomes clear that doubt concerns lack of confidence in truths. All of us crave for certainty. If we set out on a journey, we want to be sure we will arrive – but we can never be sure! All sorts of things can scupper our plans. But we have to decide whether we have sufficient confidence in them to venture forth. We set out in faith, having sufficient confidence in our knowing to justify going.

This lack of certainty has to be faced. Can we be certain of anything? Can I be certain that my money is safe in the bank, that my health will survive the day and that my wife will remain faithful?

I need also to ask myself whether my doubts are reasonable. Certainly, my worst fears could materialise, but generally I find that our bank manager can be trusted, my doctor is rightly optimistic about my health and my wife is as good as she looks! In the event, the Normandy Invasion was successful and most of

Churchill's Mulberry harbour survived the journey, weathered the storms and fulfilled its purpose.

The problem with proof

People talk very glibly about proof. Scientists in particular seem to encourage the idea of proof. What they call evidence, the press report as 'certainty' and their readers regard as proof. Concerning Christianity, atheists and agnostics say, 'Prove it to me!' Zealous Christians say to their friends that they will 'prove' to them that Christianity is true, when they mean they will present the evidence hoping to persuade them to act on it.

The search for absolute certainty is a hopeless quest in a matter of probabilities. In British law, an accused person is innocent until he is shown to be guilty 'beyond all reasonable doubt'. I sat on a jury, and having heard the evidence, we retired to reach our verdict. A persuasive juryman mapped out his reasons for thinking the accused was not guilty. I thought he made out a reasonable case, but to balance it, I tried to put forward a case for thinking he was guilty. The jury then divided six against six, and a prolonged discussion did not resolve it. So we failed to reach a verdict. The case then had to be retried, at significant cost and inconvenience to all concerned. Fortunately for everyone, it required a new jury!

Even if we had witnessed the crime in question, we still could not have been *absolutely* certain. The man could have a twin brother, he may have been framed, our eyes might have deceived us, there may be significant pieces of information that were kept from us, etc.

Getting the idea of absolute proof out of the way is fundamentally important in evaluating truth. We don't help ourselves when we talk about 'proof' in absolute terms, and we certainly don't help unbelievers. They know from common experience that people have mistaken beliefs and it is not the intensity of our passionate believing that is likely to persuade them.

Double-mindedness

If doubt is not the opposite of faith, neither is it the same as unbelief. The word comes from the Latin, *dubitare*. It means to hesitate, to be uncertain, to hover between two opinions. '...for the one who doubts is like a wave of the sea that is driven and tossed by the wind...he is double-minded man, unstable in all his ways' (James 1:6–8). Doubt immobilises us, yet it is an essential ingredient, a stopping point on our journey towards an opinion. Jesus allowed his disciples to doubt as he gradually brought them to the point where, in faith, they confessed him as Lord. He allowed them time, even respecting the doubts of Thomas, but he urged them to resolve the matter. 'Do not disbelieve, but believe' (John 20:27).

A corrupted mind

It is unusual for a thoughtful Christian to be overwhelmed suddenly by doubts after trusting in Christ for many years. Confronted by such a story, it is always worth asking what else was going on in that person's life. In my experience, there is usually a moral issue that preceded the apparently intellectual one. A prominent atheist, who had previously been the minister of a church, tried to persuade me in a radio debate that intellectual issues had led to his change of mind. When pressed specifically as to what else was going on in his life, he admitted committing adultery and to being hooked on pornography when the doubts started to flood in. The Scriptures repeatedly warn us that immorality affects our thinking (Romans 1:18, 21, 26, 28).

The Christian understanding of human fallenness is that we have become morally corrupted at a deep level. We are not totally depraved in the sense that we are as bad as we can possibly be, but totally depraved in the sense that no aspect of our lives is unaffected by human sin. As a consequence, our desires and motives are affected by self-centredness. None of us is an entirely honest broker in handling truth. We tend to see it the way we want to see it. We have motives, including financial ones and the desire to succeed. This has enormous implications for science. As we have seen, the recording and interpreting of scientific data requires entirely honest and truthful scientists. Yet none exist. We all have vested interests, and numerous examples of duplicity have been discovered in scientific reporting. Ambition, pride and complacency all come into the picture, as if knowledge wasn't difficult enough to obtain. We are both finite in terms of our ability to comprehend and corrupted in our ability to handle truth with relentless integrity.

Doubt about doubts

Doubts themselves need to be analysed and interrogated. We need to explore the doubts about our doubts. Paul talked about pulling down strongholds and every lofty idea raised up against the knowledge of God and bringing every thought captive in obedience to Christ (2 Corinthians 10:4,5). Every evangelist needs to engage with this work, and all of us need to help one another to deal with honest doubts. Pastors in their preaching have a particular responsibility here.

As followers of truth we can confront our doubts and follow the evidence wherever it leads. If it is true, it is true. It is always safe, though not always comfortable, to follow truth.

The danger of doubt

Doubt is a halfway house and the danger is that it becomes a resting place. Some pilgrims fail to progress because they find in 'Doubting Castle'[50] a stronghold to protect them, where they never need to resolve the issues. These people love to ask questions – but they ask the same questions again and again. They never move on, and their insincerity becomes increasingly apparent.

This should not surprise us. Jesus described Satan as the father of lies (John 8:44). This personification of evil sits uncomfortably in the modern mind. Yet both Old and New Testaments imply that evil has a mind of its own. It is devious, deceitful and scheming. We are told it fed doubts into the mind of Eve in the garden and tried to sow them into the mind of Christ in the wilderness. So we need to be very wary about doubts and seek to resolve them. They are a call to action. To linger in doubt reinforces it and brings about an inertia, which C.S. Lewis' 'Screwtape' would delight in.[51]

Healthy scepticism

Scepticism is not the same as cynicism. It is said that the sceptic hopes it may prove to be true while the cynic fears that it is. The cynic has given up on truth and mocks the honest seeker. But a healthy scepticism has a proper place in our quest for knowledge. Its strength is in questioning, checking, testing and verifying. As such it is an essential tool. Os Guinness put it like this: 'Like a terrier, doubt worries at weak ideas until they escape reinvigorated or collapse exhausted.'[52]

Doubt helps us resolve great issues – but then we must move on. Jesus taught, 'Seek – and you will find.' The devil says the meaning is found only in the quest, not in the conclusion. Without that diligent care and probing integrity inspired by doubt, we are liable to be misled – and will then mislead others. Francis Bacon warned, 'If a man will begin with certainties, he shall end in doubts; but if he will be content with doubts, he shall end with certainties.'[53] Doubt is open-minded about the outcome. It can lead to belief or unbelief, but as Eisenhower knew only too well in 1944, it demands a verdict. John Stott used to say that the only purpose in having an open mind is that you eventually close it on something substantial.

Conclusion

So what, then, is faith? William Lane Craig defines it like this: 'Faith in the biblical sense is trusting in what you have good reasons to think is true.' Such faith needs freedom to enquire, evaluate, test and resolve. Without such a firm foundation, faith is but a castle built on sand, a trust in what we do not have good reasons to think is true. The truth about God – whom no one has ever seen – can only be known, if God makes himself knowable. That is the uniqueness of the Christian Faith (John 1:18). In the mercy of God, the truth is there to be found.

CHAPTER 13
TIME FOR QUESTIONS

If dialogue and persuasion are central parts of the evangelist's task, and doubts are a legitimate and necessary staging post on the journey to faith, what is the place of reasoned apologetics in the weekly teaching ministry of the church?

A more fundamental question, of course, is whether unconvinced people ever come to our churches! However, such people are not just non-Christians. Many unconvinced churchgoers want Christianity to be true. They are 'would be' Christians but secretly fear it is not true. The arguments of the secular world are increasingly undermining their confidence.

Ten years ago, Church Survey UK[55] asked the question of why so many people were dropping away from church. Consolidating the responses of 14,000 people, the survey report drew five main conclusions. The first and foremost of these was the need for apologetics to be given priority in the weekly sermon. Chapter one began: 'People want churches to emphasize the many reasons why believing in God and Christianity makes sense and to challenge a doubting society.' Seventy-three per cent of respondents to the survey indicated that a growing number of people are leaving church under the false impression that 'there are no strong reasons for Christian belief'. A typical respondent said:

> The Bible speaks about...a reasoned and logical faith which is built on a firm foundation of facts and information. For a church to be vibrant and healthy, this body of evidence needs to be regularly presented and explained, so that congregations can learn and see for themselves why believing makes sense.

In Britain, anyway, the survey indicates that clergy are failing their congregations badly in this matter. It seems that while apologetic issues are often dealt with in home-group Bible studies, they are rarely addressed from the pulpit. How can that be rectified?

Is it believable?
Whether preaching doctrinally or expounding a biblical text consecutively, preachers need to imagine that they are in dialogue with their congregations. (Occasional real-life dialogues, where the preacher invites questions following a sermon, would be a great help. However, many preachers do not feel confident enough to do this, and we will return to that problem shortly.)

Whether or not the preacher invites questions, they would do well to imagine during the preparation of the sermon what questions this passage or doctrine might raise in the minds of unbelievers. Having identified likely questions, the preacher can then consider how best to address them.

Acknowledge the difficulties
Recently, in my travels, I heard an excellent sermon on Abraham.

It was well-prepared, relevant and thoughtful. It just failed to make any reference at all to 'the elephant in the room'. If the preacher had allowed just one question from the congregation, surely it would have been about the great ages of the patriarchs. Abraham himself we were told fell on his face and laughed. 'Shall a child be born to a man who is a hundred years old? Shall Sarah, who is ninety … bear a child?'(Genesis 17:17). Sarah went on to live 127 years and Abraham lived to 175 (Genesis 23:1; 25:7).

Now, it is one thing that the preacher did not offer a good explanation of these extraordinary ages, but not to acknowledge the problem at all was a serious error of judgement. What did he imagine his congregation was thinking? Does he want them to stop using their brains?

Pointing toward explanations

Well, he may have started by acknowledging that the ages recorded in Genesis seem extraordinary to us but yield to no simple explanation. That anyway would have shown that he was not a gullible twit, who hadn't even noticed the difficulty. But he could have said much more. He could have pointed out that these ages, however they were understood, presumably did not seem extraordinary to the writer or the original readers! Apparently, the ancient Egyptians saw 110 and 120 as the 'ideal' ages of a long life.

Derek Kidner, a former warden at Tyndale House, Cambridge and writing some fifty years ago, packed his Tyndale commentary on Genesis with wise comments. On this matter, he made the simple observation that most of the ages of the patriarchs are twice what we would expect. So Abraham arrived in Canaan aged seventy-five, rather than thirty-eight. Sarah went into the menopause age ninety, instead of forty-five. The ages of their deaths seem twice what we might expect. She died aged 127 years, rather than sixty-four. Abraham died at 175 years rather than eighty-seven years. Abraham is explicitly recorded as dying at a 'a good old age, an old man and full of years' (Genesis 25:8) which is probably the more precise statement of his age!

Sixty years ago, my grandfather died at the age of seventy-three years. He was the only one of my grandparents to live long enough to meet their grandchildren. 'Three score years and ten' seemed a good age then. But today in the UK, a healthy 20-year-old can expect on *average* to live into his eighties. We have a delightful custom in Britain where the Queen sends a message of greeting to everyone who reaches their 100th birthday. But this is no longer a rarity! In 2012, there were over 13,000 such people. One in 1,000 of these centenarians now survives to 110, and thirty people in the world have had documented ages of 115. We are not really sure why people are living longer today – there is no simple explanation. A balanced diet, hygiene, central heating and immunisations all play a part. Curative medicine, whether by surgery or antibiotics, has a much smaller role. But the process of ageing itself is poorly understood and some scientists think it may not be essential to grow old, though the cure for ageing is not 'around the corner' and it would be very problematic if it was!

So we don't know what to make of the great ages of the patriarchs, but you cannot read the story without thinking about it. Now, I may have offered more detail here than would fit easily into a sermon about Abraham. But some such comment, at least to acknowledge the unresolved difficulties, should be made before moving on to more interesting and relevant matters, such as Abraham's faith. Otherwise, the whole story appears fanciful, which it isn't.

Tuning-in to the questions

Now, I sympathise with the vulnerability of inexperienced preachers, but surely, part of their preparation time should be given over to anything in the sermon that raises a legitimate question. I am not talking here about preachers who prepare their sermons on the back of an envelope on Sunday morning over breakfast. I am talking about preachers who take the task seriously and prepare diligently. That should include identifying defeater arguments.

What are 'defeater' arguments?

A 'defeater' is a belief, which if proved true, would imply, directly or indirectly, that another belief was false. The preacher gives his or her attention to what they think their hearers should reasonably believe on the basis of the sermon. They are in the 'belief' business, so they must give their attention to defeater arguments, otherwise their audience will be left with no reason to believe that what they are saying is actually true. It is difficult to imagine a more fundamental failure on behalf of a preacher.

But in the UK, anyway, at least until recently, apologetics was not even being taught in theological colleges. They devote time to doctrine, liturgy, pastoral studies, ethics and church history – to name but a few – but rarely do they study apologetics. Hence, people commence their years in ministry substantially unprepared to do that most basic task of all, persuading their congregations that Christianity is true and that they, their families, friends and work colleagues need to hear sound reasons why they should all become Christians.

Where to begin?

Many congregations serve coffee after their Sunday morning

services. Now, the person who gave the welcome and introduced the service can be given the job of standing at the door to shake hands with people as they leave, while the preacher can be set up in a corner with a cup of coffee and a circle of chairs around them for anyone who has questions to come and talk, along with any others who want to listen in.

(I should flag up in passing the alarming phenomenon that the congregations of most British churches are predominantly female (commonly 60-80 per cent), but when it comes to seminars, lectures or conferences on 'apologetic' subjects, the attendance is often more than 80 per cent male. This is very striking. The needs of men seem to be quite different in this area. The British population is about 31 million men and 32 million women. Any serious deviation from such proportions in church suggests that something is very wrong in the way that church is going about its task. As a consequence, this means pastorally that huge numbers of Christian women will never find a Christian husband.)

If, by inviting questions, it sounds as though I am suggesting that Christian education be taken seriously – YEP, I am! I realise that preaching is more than teaching – but it isn't less! The preacher must take teaching seriously. By starting in this easy way, preachers can explore the difficulties people have with Christian belief in this weekly, small-group session after the sermon. If the preachers can't answer their questions, they can frankly admit it and say that they will do some 'research' and get back to the questioner by email during the week. This is not rocket science! Little by little, they will grow in confidence and be able more accurately to anticipate the questions their sermons might provoke.

When they have more confidence, they might then try, if only occasionally, perhaps monthly on a planned and advertised basis, to have a fifteen-minute period for public questions after the sermon. These could be written on cards and collected by someone who could quickly collate them and feed them back to the preacher after the next song. Alternatively, they can be texted through to a given phone number, or they can be spoken into a standing or a roving microphone.

The benefits of this approach are huge. The odds are that any given question arising directly from the talk, will also be forming in the minds of other people in the congregation. So lots of people wake up at this point and think, 'Now, that is a good question! How will it be answered?' As a result, when they are asked a similar question by a friend, they will remember the way it was answered in church – both the manner and the substance of the answer.

If the question is outside the remit of the sermon, the preacher can politely decline to answer it off the cuff and invite the individual to chat about it afterwards.

Another major benefit is that this will add enormous credibility to the preacher. They are shown not to be glib, and do not pretend to be able to answer every question. They welcome questions and will go away and work on the ones they can't answer. The exercise will underline the importance that truth matters and that Christianity stands or falls on matters of truth and offers substantial answers to important questions.

A question panel?

For the pastor who is apprehensive about this, why not set up a panel? Many churches have within their congregation members talented in a wide range of fields. So why not set up a diverse panel of clergy and leading lay people to answer questions from the congregation? This could be done instead of a sermon, perhaps every three months or on a weekday evening. A scientist, a businessman, a professional person and a clergy person, offering expertise in a range of disciplines, could each offer an answer to the questions, putting their own perspectives on the issues raised. A chairperson with a relaxed and easy manner could coordinate the event.

The BBC have been broadcasting such events for political questions on both radio and television on a weekly basis for a great many years. They remain two of the most enduring and successful BBC broadcasts!

A regular course?

For several years now, my home church has put on autumn and spring Reasonable Faith courses. Taking our inspiration from the work of William Lane Craig, we tackle two subjects per week over tea or coffee served with home-made cakes on Sunday afternoons. We have built up a team of speakers and this term we are due to tackle the cosmological, fine-tuning and moral arguments for God, the archaeological and historical evidences for Old Testament stories, issues of science and faith, Islamic and Christian views of Scripture, the application of ethical systems, the earliest evidences of Christian faith, the life and times of C.S.Lewis (with guest lecturer Alister McGrath), a personal testimony, and finishing the term with a panel discussion.

Speakers are generally allowed twenty minutes, followed by ten minutes for questions, finishing within the hour, and numbers attending vary between fifteen and fifty. All our talks are recorded and available on our church website.[56]

As an outreach event?

A small and struggling local church near the health centre

where I worked were having great difficulty getting local people to come to church, and they seemed very short of money and talents in their congregation. Someone thought of having an 'Any Questions' event. So they invited a lawyer, who attended a nearby church, a town councillor who was also a local shopkeeper, me as a local family doctor and their own pastor to form the panel.

The event was advertised by flyers delivered to all the local houses and by personal distribution from church members. Timed for 7.30 p.m. one weekday evening, the Question Time was followed at 9p.m. by refreshments, mainly tea, cakes and biscuits. The format was simple, the event was unthreatening, and it was easy for them to welcome friends from their local community.

They had never before experienced such a crowd of people turning up at church! It started with a warm welcome from the event organiser (but no prayer – they wisely did that beforehand). The questions were wide-ranging; they included local affairs and medical matters, but the opportunities to speak wisely and helpfully about the truth and relevance of Christian belief kept occurring spontaneously. The atmosphere was friendly, cheerful and welcoming – it was to my mind a great outreach event.

Now, you couldn't pull off an event like that every month, but what if every church did it once a year?

The dangers of manipulation

The question of whether or not to pray publicly at such an event raises a related matter of great importance: that is, the need to make 'outsiders' feel comfortable and at ease during our public services. As a bloke, and speaking on behalf of a great many blokes, as is evident from their behaviour in church, many of us do not like drawing attention to ourselves, and we certainly don't like being trapped and manipulated from the front. So we do not, in general, like doing the actions to children's choruses or any other embarrassing activity. To be asked to put a hand around the man sitting next to me, whom I have never seen before, and asking him to reveal his deepest prayer needs to me is really 'not on'. And yet many churches regularly embarrass their congregations. What you might do in a church members' meeting midweek is quite different from what you can get away with in your Sunday public services, unless you want to drive fringe members and outsiders away. Jesus taught, 'Whatever you wish that others would do for you, do also to them' (Matthew 7:12). We need to put ourselves in the outsider's place.

So Christ's 'Golden Rule' extends to entering other people's thoughts and emotions. We must try to address the questions they might ask and appreciate the feelings they might have, if they are going to be able to hear what we are saying. Jesus prayed, 'As you sent me into the world, so I have sent them into the world' (John 17:18). How did Jesus come into our world? Archbishop Michael Ramsey commented on this text that we must therefore 'enter the doubts of the doubting, the questions of the questioning and the loneliness of those who have lost their way'.

CHAPTER 14
TELLING HIS STORY

———◦———

It doesn't happen very often, but just occasionally it does: someone in the middle of a conversation spontaneously asks a really basic question. 'What is it that you Christians believe?' or 'Can you explain Christianity to me?' Chappo used to say, 'The reason you don't get asked it very much is because God knows you would only muck it up!' If we could explain the gospel clearly and confidently, we might find more Spirit-led opportunities to talk about it.

I have a sneaking feeling that most Christians think, 'Of course, I could explain it.' But when you actually ask them to do so, it is not long before they get thoroughly knotted up. Chappo had some memorable advice here. 'There is no substitute for rehearsed spontaneity!'

It must be a good idea to have a clear framework to use, a logical structure that starts off at the right place, has a clear sequence of ideas, has definite aims and anticipates some of the pitfalls you might encounter. This can be used as a short explanation or as a backdrop at the start of an interactive dialogue. In any conversation of integrity, what you say in answering a question necessarily shapes the next question. We want to lead people to Jesus, not talk them into a ditch.

Memorising a framework can be usefully worked on in small groups. I would suggest perhaps five or six people meet to rehearse their spontaneity together. They need to be given notice that they will be asked to explain the gospel without notes, within a two-minute period. If they agree to such demands, and having committed the group to think and pray about the matter, let them take it in turns to have a go and then discuss together how well the others thought they did, before inviting the next member to have a go, learning from the other person's mistakes.

Where do you start?

The immediate problem is the opening sentence! Do you start with sin and then talk about the Saviour? Do you talk about the church and hope to introduce the gospel? Do you start with the Bible – and if so, where? Some might launch off about the Pope or Richard Dawkins and still hope to bring it round to the gospel (that journey is liable to take the scenic route!).

The idea of allowing each person only two minutes is, of course, to focus their minds. The further removed your starting point is, the less likely you are to get across the ground you hope to cover. But that assumes you know the territory and where you hope to finish. It usually becomes clear in thirty seconds whether you a) have any hope of reaching home base or b) whether you have any idea what home base might even look like.

Of course, a brief summary cannot hope to comprehensively cover everything, but knowing where to start, what key points to flag up en route, and knowing where you want to get to are all important in setting up a good discussion.

Consider the central thrust

For many Christians, the central thrust will be 'The Bible'! Their favourite version will be opened at the earliest possible moment, and they will start reading from it. Their core belief is that the Bible is the Word of God, and people need to hear the Word of God because it has divine power to reach into people's hearts and souls (Hebrews 4:12).

A moment's reflection will show that the first Christians did not do it like that! The New Testament for them wasn't even written, and while the Old Testament scriptures were used in evangelising the Jews, who accepted their authority, these ancient documents were largely unknown to the Gentiles. The earliest Christians clearly did not go out proclaiming the Bible. Certainly, Jesus rebuked the Pharisees for not knowing their Old Testament scriptures, but neither he nor the apostles invited people to trust a book. Rather, they proclaimed a person and saw Jesus as the living Word who invited people to follow him.

I hear someone say, 'You cannot talk about Jesus without referring directly or indirectly to the Bible.' Certainly, everything we know about Jesus is found in the Bible! But that does not mean we should use the Bible as an authoritative book which we are asking unbelievers to trust. Unlike Islam and many cults, we are not peddling a book. Believing the Bible to be inspired Scripture flows out of our prior convictions about Jesus and his apostles. It may be an authoritative book for us, but it is certainly not seen like that by unbelievers.

We are not, therefore, promoting a circular argument. Many Christians fall into this trap. They justify Jesus from the Bible and the Bible from Jesus, and are quite unable to see their way out of it. Unbelievers, of course, are quite unable to see their way into it! If, in your two-minute presentation of Christianity, you present this circular argument, rest assured that the unbeliever listening to you will quickly spot it and point it out. You have firmly tied the cart in front of the horse, when it should be pulled along behind it. In contrast, the early Christians presented a linear argument from Christ as an historical person:

> Paul, a servant of Christ Jesus, called to be an apostle, set apart for the gospel of God, which he promised beforehand through his prophets in the holy Scriptures, concerning his Son, who was descended from David according to the flesh and was declared to be the Son of God in power according to the Spirit of holiness by his resurrection from the dead, Jesus Christ our Lord, through whom ...
> (Romans 1:1–5, ESV)

OK. Paul would have difficulty doing it in two minutes, but the line of argument is clear. It is a linear argument from historical facts, albeit events that were prophesied in OT scriptures.

Hear how he addresses the intellectual Athenians: 'God ... now ... commands all people everywhere to repent, because he has fixed a day on which he will judge the world in righteousness by a man whom he has appointed; and of this has given assurance to all by raising him from the dead' (Acts 17:30–31).

Or Peter at Pentecost, 'Jesus of Nazareth, a man attested to you by God with mighty works and wonders ... that God did through him in your midst, as you yourselves know...God raised him up...Let all the house of Israel therefore know for certain that God has made him both Lord and Christ, this Jesus whom you crucified' (Acts 2:22,24,36).

As Festus reported to King Agrippa, '[The Jews] had certain points of dispute with [Paul] about their own religion and about a certain Jesus, who was dead, but whom Paul asserted to be alive' (Acts 25:19).

And Paul before Festus and Agrippa, 'so I stand here testifying both to small and great, saying nothing but what the prophets and Moses said would come to pass: that the Christ must suffer and that, by being the first to rise from the dead, he would proclaim light both to our people and to the Gentiles...For the king knows about these things...For I am persuaded that none of these things has escaped his notice, for this has not been done in a corner' (Acts 26:22–26).

The apostles proclaimed the historic facts of Christ. Yes, they used the Old Testament prophecies to support their case, but the facts which they asserted were historical events to which they were witnesses.

So in replacing Judas to make up 'The Twelve', Peter said the candidate must be someone who 'accompanied us during all the time that the Lord Jesus went in and out among us...one of these men must become with us a witness to his resurrection' (Acts 1:21,22).

Now, this is most important in telling the gospel story. It relates to specific events in space-time history, summarised in that earliest of creeds (1Corinthians 15:3–5) and witnessed by hundreds which, if untrue, means 'We are even found to be misrepresenting God, because we testified about God that he raised Christ, whom he did not raise if it is true that the dead are not raised...And if Christ has not been raised, your faith is futile and... we are of all people most to be pitied'(1Corinthians 15:15–19).

So the early Christians made out their case from the

known, witnessed facts of history. They did not hide behind an authoritative book, which they trusted as Scripture. Christ's deeds and sayings were committed to memory, but the New Testament was not assembled for a long while. They were asking people to have faith in a person, not in a book.

This means that we can use the New Testament to present the gospel story, but we do so not as 'the Bible', but as the collection of historical documents which bear witness to the Christ events.

Now this fundamental idea will affect the way we present Christ. We will avoid such phrases as, 'The Bible says...' and we will readily say, 'Jesus said... Jesus did... Jesus was...' How will we justify such statements? Mostly with reference to the Gospel narratives. For example, 'Jesus said in the Sermon on the Mount recorded in Matthew's Gospel...' or 'Jesus said in his parable about the Good Samaritan in Luke's account...' or 'One of Jesus' highly memorable sayings about the things we personally value was "Where your treasure is, there will your heart be also"' etc.

The figure of Christ is well-documented. We know his values, his character, his style, his deeds, his claims and many of his sayings. We can in 'broad brush' assume this documentation. Occasionally we will be asked to justify this. But even then, in evangelism it is the 'broad brush' picture of Christ in the Gospels that we need to proclaim, not arguing the details of a particular point.

Of course, if they offer a wholesale scepticism about the Gospel manuscripts, we will have to take a step back and discuss their general credibility. I would provoke them by offering them a copy of a Gospel and invite them to cross out every part they felt could not be trusted. We could then discuss the rest!

Our aim, then, is to present Christ as he saw himself and encourage people to first of all learn about him and then to trust him.

But where to start?

If our focus is to present Christ, is he the first person we should mention? Looking at the texts quoted above, it is very difficult to say much about Christ without discussing the existence and purposes of God. And that for many people is the real stumbling block. They don't believe in God.

Now, if Jesus reveals God, there is a case to be made that in presenting Jesus we can leave him to persuade unbelievers that God exists. For instance, the resurrection of Jesus directly implies the existence of God. That was certainly the route I personally took. I was agnostic about God until I was confronted by the person of Christ and the compelling evidence for his resurrection.

But certainly in our more secular world today, we probably need to say something about the reasonableness of belief in God before we can talk about God's revelation of himself in Jesus. C.S. Lewis was not alone in first coming to believe in God and then finding him coming into focus in the historic and risen Christ. The great challenge for him was to believe in God. It was a much smaller step to then believe in Christ.

Today, of course, we can marshal some strong arguments for God's existence, aided significantly by the findings of modern science. The creation of the universe from nothing some 13.8 billion years ago is very difficult to understand if there was no agency to bring it about.

The remarkable fine-tuning of the universe, in the first moments of the Big Bang when the laws of physics were established, speaks powerfully about intentional design.

The moral argument is as powerful today as it ever was. If there are no consequences, all rules are arbitrary 'house rules' of human invention. Moral relativism has to be the order of the day unless morality can be grounded in the nature of the God who made us.

So we would be wise at the outset to affirm the existence of God and indicate some of our reasons for being at least open-minded about his existence, before presenting the case for Christ.

Talking about the cross

When we start talking about Jesus, many Christians will rush into talk about his atoning death on the cross. Albeit well-intentioned, this assumes too much. Unless your reference to the moral argument has unpacked the nature of our alienation from the God to whom we are accountable, we are likely to be putting a quite indigestible number of questions on the table to be consumed in one hurried meal.

We have to talk about 'sin' before we can talk about salvation, but we cannot talk about Christ's death for sin until we have talked meaningfully about God's incarnation in Christ. Look at the way Paul recorded his evangelism in Corinth: 'For I decided to know nothing among you except Jesus Christ and him crucified' (1Corinthians 2:2).

How did Paul proclaim the 'testimony of God'? Through telling them about Jesus Christ. And it was not until they had a firm grasp as to who Jesus was in terms of the testimony of God that he could then go on to talk about the significance of his death. The important thing about the crucifixion was not the cross but the person who hung on it. Back to my friend Chappo; he used to make the point that 'the cross is not the first statement of the gospel'. Certainly, you cannot preach the gospel without discussing the meaning of Christ's death for our sins. It is central but first you must discuss his identity and claims, before you can discuss the significance of his death.

Developing an easily memorable outline

Chappo taught me this very simple structure to explain Christian belief and I have used it ever since:

God–Man–God–What if I do–What if I don't

It is infinitely adaptable. Chappo often used it as a brief talk before inviting questions at Dialogue Supper Parties. How short can you make it? Here is how I might use it if allowed some thirty seconds:

> We believe in God – for a variety of good reasons. We believe that humankind was made in his image, but has failed to live as God intended. We have become lost and cut off from God. Christians believe that God has come after us, uniquely intervening in history to rescue us. Jesus shows us how to live, and through his death and resurrection offers us forgiveness and the possibility of knowing God personally. If we reject his love and forgiveness, he will hold us accountable for the way we have lived.

Here is a three-minute version:

(God) We believe in God for good reasons. For instance, he is the only credible explanation for the universe, both in its creation out of nothing and its fine-tuning for intelligent life. We also believe in the reality of good and evil, which must be grounded ultimately in the goodness of God. The character of God has been revealed in the historic person of Jesus, whom men crucified but God vindicated by raising him from the dead.

(Man) We believe humankind was intended to live in a

close and dependent relationship with God and reflecting his goodness, but we have declared our independence of him and live our lives in isolation from him, following our own desires. Hence the mess we are in.

(God) God, whose ultimate character is love, has set out on a rescue mission to bring us back into relationship with himself. In the historic person of Christ, he has entered our world, declared his purposes, but more than that, has carried in himself the judgement that our independence deserves. Christ's death, at the hands of wicked men, was experienced in our place, so that he might hold out to us the offer of forgiveness, no matter what dreadful things we might have done. Through his death and resurrection, he calls us to turn away from everything we know to be wrong, and live a new life walking in Christ's footsteps, empowered by his Spirit.

(What if we do?) If we turn to God and accept his offer of forgiveness, we can start afresh, redeeming our days by loving God first and foremost, and inspired by him to love our neighbour with the same passion that used to drive our love for ourselves. This spiritual life, allowing God to be God over us, does not end in our death, but continues in his presence into eternity. If God made this extraordinary world, why should we think he cannot make another?

(What if we don't?) If we continue to ignore God's purposes for us, we will be held accountable for our actions. In turning away from God, we are destined to be separated from him in eternity.

This three-minute presentation is still very brief and can certainly be improved upon, but we must each find a way of expressing our beliefs that is true to God, the gospel and ourselves. It can be used in answer to a direct enquiry about Christian belief. It can used to provoke questions and form the backdrop for a discussion, or it can provide the headings of a much fuller response when opportunity allows. It could easily form the basis of five talks!

The important thing about the outline summary is that it is easily memorable and therefore gives you confidence. You start in the right place. You talk about your belief in God before discussing his coming in Christ. You consider Christ's character and claims before discussing the significance of his death and resurrection. You talk about the choices we all have to make before discussing the ultimate destinies to which they lead.

In particular, grasping the structure *God, Man, God, What if I do, What if I don't* is simple enough to keep the Christian on track (and it doesn't require a paper napkin and a pencil to illustrate!).

CHAPTER 15
BURIED IN POMPEII

———•———

I have highlighted the dangers of Christians presenting their faith in a circular argument from an authoritative book. The challenge today is to present Christian belief as a linear argument from history. The first Christians had no choice in this! It was sometime before they had any documents to work from and it was over 300 years before there was agreement as to which books should form the New Testament, though the earliest drafts of the Gospels may well have been copied and circulated before AD50.

As Luke wrote, 'Inasmuch as many have undertaken to compile a narrative of the things that have been accomplished among us, just as those who from the beginning were eyewitnesses and ministers of the word have delivered them to us, it seemed good to me also, having followed all things closely for some time past, to write an orderly account for you, most excellent Theophilus, that you may have certainty concerning the things you have been taught.' (Luke 1:1–4).

The Jews had a strong reliance on 'oral transmission' and

Jesus the Jew taught in highly rhythmic and memorable sayings, which retain their rhythm even in translation. For example, 'The Sabbath was made for man, not man for the Sabbath' (Mark 2:27). Or look at the structure of his parables, such as the Good Samaritan, told with great economy of words, in just six rhythmic sentences (Luke 10:30–35). Jesus intended his sayings to be remembered.

After a generation, they were able to accumulate authoritative Gospels and Letters to quote from and refer to in their evangelism, but they could only handle them as historical documents to support what they were saying. If they had them at all, they had them as separate documents. Christ's parables and sayings carried their own intrinsic authority.

It was a long time – and a gradual process – before the New Testament collection was formed and widely accepted as apostolic and definitive for the growing church. In our post-Christian culture, the Bible's authority as a book is long gone. While not denying its inner power, the New Testament today, as in the first century, carries only its historical and intrinsic credibility among unbelievers. Neither they nor we could pretend that saying 'The Bible says...' puts an end to any argument.

I want in these next three chapters to ask you to travel with me and explore the clues that enable us to imagine how the Gospel spread in that first generation.

Historical evidence

When I first read the New Testament in my late teens I was, like my parents, an unbeliever. I read it only as a product of history, making no assumptions about its reliability. I was certainly not going to take a blind leap of faith into believing its contents. What background reading I did was to help me understand the historicity of these documents, and I still remember many of my first impressions from that initial reading.

For instance, while I had not at that age read the Koran, I had expected that the New Testament would be that sort of document– full of somewhat disjointed, religious assertions with very little narrative and no rational argumentation. I expected to find in the New Testament dogma and doctrine on every page and unjustified dictats as to what I 'ought' to believe.

So my first great surprise was to find a record of events and the stories of very real people caught up in those events. Here was a strong historical narrative with compelling pictures of individuals. And this was not merely the case for the leading figures in the story. For instance, I just loved those disjointed bits at the end of the letters. Here was Paul, as it were, 'off camera' with the sound still recording. Here are captured irrelevant pleasantries, intriguing comments, telling asides... the very stuff of history. Every historian just loves stumbling on a batch of old letters! Nothing takes you closer to events than eyewitness, contemporary accounts.

Consider the end of Paul's letter to the Christians in Rome, written from Corinth in around AD57. There are fascinating glimpses of his past, future and present plans: '...I no longer have any room for work in these regions... I hope to see you in passing as I go to Spain... At present ...I am going to Jerusalem bringing aid ...for the poor' (Romans 15:23ff).

Paul goes on to send greetings to more than thirty individuals in Rome, most of whom we know nothing about. Having never been to Rome, it is a wonder that Paul knew anything about them either. Yet he seems to know them well, so he must have met them on his travels, like the two heading the list - the dynamic duo Priscilla and Aquila, whom he met in Corinth. We shall consider them in detail later. Epaenetus, we learn, was his first convert in Asia (Turkey). Andronicus and Junia were his 'kinsmen', which probably meant they were fellow Jews, and they had been imprisoned with him. Junia may well have been female. Paul wrote: 'They are outstanding among the apostles, and they were in Christ before I was' (Romans 16:7NIV). F.F. Bruce commented that this 'probably means they were not merely well known to the apostles but were apostles themselves (in a wider sense of the word) and eminent ones at that. They had been Christians from a very early date, since before Paul's own conversion...their title to apostleship may even have been based on their having seen the risen Christ'[57] (see Acts 1:21–26). But we know nothing about 'my beloved Stachys' (Romans16:9). Herodion was a kinsman, presumably a fellow Jew. Rufus' mother 'has been a mother to me as well' (Romans 16:13), and so it goes on. As he sends them his greetings, he also sends them greetings from seven other people. They include his fellow-worker Timothy; Lucius, Jason and Sosipater 'my kinsmen' (Romans 16:21) and Tertius who actually wrote the letter, which Paul had dictated and which Phoebe delivered (Romans 16:1). He then mentions Gaius, who set an example for all Christians, 'whose hospitality I and the whole church here enjoy' (Romans 16:23NIV).

Before closing, he sends greetings from 'Erastus, the city treasurer' (Romans 16:23). This name occurs three times in the New Testament (Romans 16:23; Acts 19:22; 2Timothy 4:20), which could all refer to the same person.

The Greek word used here implies a city official, a public steward, treasurer or manager. In the Latin of ancient Rome, he was an 'aedile', an elected magistrate who was responsible for public buildings, streets, markets, festivals and games. This was an unpaid role for wealthy young men who were aspiring politicians, and they were elected for a one-year term.

 Paul was writing from Corinth, where in 1929 a Latin inscription on a marble pavement slab was discovered, dating from the first century. It reads, ERASTVS PRO: AEDILIT: S: P: STRAVIT, which was Latin shorthand for: 'Erastus, commissioner for public works, laid this pavement at his own expense'. S and P stand for Sua Pecunia – 'his own money'. It is entirely reasonable to conclude this was Paul's man.[58]

Before we consider Priscilla and Aquila, and as a backdrop to them, let's first visit another couple in another place, who were almost their contemporaries.

Is there evidence of Christianity in Pompeii?

The eruption of Vesuvius in AD79 caused the cities of Pompeii and Herculaneum to be frozen in time. The first treasures to be dug out of the ashes and the solidified lava surfaced in 1748 and since then a slow, laborious excavation has been producing fascinating detail about life in these Roman cities.

In 1862, in a building opposite a brothel, there was discovered an enigmatic graffiti incorporating the word '*christianos*'. It was written in charcoal, and within a short time had been washed away. However, two experts had made tracings of it. It is thought to have been an inscription from Aramaic, yielding the sentence: 'A strange mind has overtaken A who is now being held as a prisoner among the Christians.' Whether or not this possibly means that someone whose initial was 'A' stopped using the brothel as a result of becoming a Christian, it anyway remains the earliest known reference to 'Christians' outside the New Testament.[59]

The next indication came in the discovery of graffiti in 1929 crudely etched on a doorpost of the home of a baker, showing the earliest known (pre-AD79) SATOR square. This fascinating Latin palindrome has been known for centuries and has been found in many places across Europe and elsewhere. Two English examples in Manchester and Cirencester date from the Roman era. Most are found in locations associated with Christianity. Ten have been found in Roman ruins.

A palindrome can be read in four directions: left to right, top to bottom, right to left and bottom to top. Four of these words have understood meanings. ROTAS means 'wheels', OPERA means 'work', TENET means 'keeps', and SATOR means 'founder', while AREPO is unknown and may have been created as the reverse of OPERA just to complete the puzzle. It seems, therefore, that the words have no clear meaning other than being a just a teasing arrangement of letters. But was it an anagram?

```
R  O  T  A  S
O  P  E  R  A
T  E  N  E  T
A  R  E  P  O
S  A  T  O  R
```

Anagrams are endlessly amusing and can present all sorts of possibilities, yet no good explanation was put forward until the 1920s. Then it was shown that the letters can be written as a cross of two words, *Paternoster* – 'our father'– with four letters left over, two As and two Os, which of course in Greek could be alpha and omega. "'I am the Alpha and the Omega," says the Lord God, "who is, and who was, and who is to come, the Almighty'" (Revelation 1:8; see Isaiah 44:6), though Revelation is thought to have been written later. A further possibility is that the T may have been intended to represent the cross, as on either side of every T in the square, horizontally or vertically, is an A and an O.

There is just one unrepeated letter in the square, which is N in the centre. This means that both *Paternosters* have to be read in the form of a cross, sharing the same N at the crux. This would be far and away the earliest evidence of Christians using a cross as their symbol.

The name of God

In Latin writing, as we have seen in the inscription concerning Erastus, a single letter often signifies a word or name. It is therefore quite probable that they saw the letter N as representing '*nomen*', the Latin for 'name', indicating for them the name of God. The Jews knew only too well the third commandment, 'You shall not misuse the name of the LORD your God...'(Exodus 20:7). They understood Yahweh (YHWH) to be God's personal name and treated it with the greatest respect. He was not a remote, unknown deity but the holy, creator God who had disclosed himself to them. But God had now revealed himself more fully in the coming of the Jewish Messiah, Jesus.

This is not far-fetched as the second line of the *Paternoster* prayer taught by Jesus highlights, as its first petition, 'Hallowed be your Name', meaning, 'May your name be honoured.' James, Christ's brother, writing around AD45–49, referred to Jesus Christ as 'the honourable name by which you were called' (James 2:7). Paul wrote about Christ being raised 'far above all rule and authority and power and dominion, above every name that is named not only in this age but also in the one to come' (Ephesians 1:21). This emphasis on the Name was again highlighted by Paul in a remarkable, early Christian poem or hymn, written in six rhythmic stanzas. This may have been originally written in Aramaic and come from Jerusalem, but presumably it was being recited or sung in Rome, when he wrote to the Philippians around AD62. It gives us deep insights into the earliest understandings of Christ:

Though he was in the form of God,
he did not count equality with God
a thing to be grasped,

But made himself nothing,
taking the form of a servant,
being born in the likeness of men.

And being found in human form,
he humbled himself by becoming obedient
to the point of death, even death on a cross.

Therefore God has highly exalted him
and bestowed on him the name
that is above every name,

So that at the name of Jesus
every knee should bow,
in heaven and on earth and under the earth,

And every tongue confess
that Jesus Christ is Lord,
to the glory of God the Father.

(Philippians 2:5–11)

To the Jews, the name above every name was the name of God (Yahweh). To say that Jesus had the highest name was to accord him with the highest honour, now represented by 'N' in the centre of both the Paternoster cross and SATOR square.

There does not seem anything forced about this interpretation and the likelihood of it being a chance finding is utterly remote. How did they manage to construct this? I think the inventor must have intentionally started with '*Paternoster*', and played with it until he formed the Sator Square. How did they manage to interpret its meaning nearly two thousand years later? Surely, the single N was the pivotal clue in resolving it.

Whilst '*Paternoster*' could have had Jewish origins, the fatherhood of God was not a central idea to them –but it was, of course, for the Christians! The New Testament refers to God as 'father' over 250 times; 165 times are within the four Gospels. Jesus had taught them the parable of the Lost Son, who came home saying, 'Father, I have sinned against heaven and against you...' as his father ran out to embrace him (Luke15:11–32). He taught them to pray to God as Father (Matthew 6:9), which was echoed by Paul, who wrote, 'You have received the Spirit of adoption as sons, by whom we cry "Abba! Father!"' (Romans 8:15). Remembering that many of the earliest Christians were themselves slaves, consider what may be Paul's earliest surviving letter, written around AD49:

> Because you are sons, God has sent the Spirit of his Son into our hearts, crying 'Abba, Father!' So you are no longer a slave, but a son, and if a son, then an heir through God.
> (Galatians 4:6,7).

The intimate, forgiving, liberating and loving Fatherhood of God was right at the centre of Christian beliefs.

But why the code?

When Paul visited Thessalonica in around AD49, the Jews started a riot. Luke records that the crowd were shouting, 'These men who have turned the world upside down have come here also...and they are all acting against the decrees of Caesar, saying that there is another king, Jesus' (Acts 17:5–9). Suetonius reports that riots among Jews in Rome occurred at that time 'on account of someone called Chrestus'.

Fifteen years later, when Nero was emperor, there was an intense persecution of Christians. They were made scapegoats for the great fire of Rome. The Roman historian Tacitus wrote:

> Nero had self-acknowledged Christians arrested. Then on their information, large numbers of others were condemned – not so much for incendiarism as for their anti-social tendencies. Dressed in animal skins, they were torn to pieces by dogs or crucified or made into torches to be ignited after dark...Nero provided his Gardens for the spectacle.[60]

These were dangerous days. They had every reason to keep

a low profile and use this highly ambiguous secret code for identification purposes. Both Peter and Paul are thought to have died under Nero's tyranny at that time.

A second SATOR square has been found in Pompeii. This one was on a column in the Palaestra, next to the arena. In AD63, a severe earthquake had shaken Pompeii, causing colossal damage to the city and it is thought that the square on the column preceded the earthquake! Consequently, the idea that it was a Christian symbol was undermined, as it was thought by many scholars to be most unlikely that Christianity could actually have reached Pompeii so early. However, there are good reasons to think it had.

Luke tells us that in the spring of (probably) AD60, he and Paul eventually arrived together in Italy aboard an Alexandrian ship, which had wintered in Malta and was therefore probably bringing in the first supply of grain that year (Acts 28:11). Their previous one, which had been wrecked at Malta, had carried 'in all 276 persons in the ship' and Luke records they had had to throw the wheat into the sea to lighten it (Acts 27:36-38). This sea journey is described vividly by Luke, who was an eye witness of the events (Acts 27). It is seen as the finest account of sea-faring to survive from the first century. Egypt was Rome's main supplier of wheat, and these huge grain ships travelled regularly from Alexandria to the Roman port of Puteoli (modern Pozzuoli), near Naples. Seneca recorded seeing large crowds assembling on the breakwater to see these great ships come in.[61] This was just thirty miles from Pompeii – and when they arrived in AD60, Paul and Luke were met by Christians:

> … There we found brothers and were invited to stay with them for seven days. And so we came to Rome. And the brothers

there, when they heard about us, came as far as the Forum of
Appius and Three Taverns to meet us …
(Acts 28:13–16)

Puteoli was a major trading centre and also the main port for
Pompeii. As we shall see shortly, importing wheat to the Bay
of Naples makes an interesting link to the man who was head
of a Pompeian bakery. The Forum and the Three Taverns were
two well-known resting points on the much used Appian Way
at distances of thirty-three and forty-three miles from Rome.
It therefore looks as though two different parties had set out to
meet Paul.

So Christians were evidently motivated to travel thirty to forty
miles from Rome to meet Paul to welcome and accompany him.
The word of his arrival had clearly gone out and we are left with no
good reason to think that Christians from Pompeii didn't make
the effort to visit Paul at Puteoli, particularly when they had the
luxury of being able to sail across the bay on regular cargo boats,
collecting, among other things, grain for their bread. Nor can we
imagine Paul losing any opportunity in Puteoli to preach and to
teach the gospel during his week there.

Why on the doorpost?

All of Christ's apostles and all the early converts to Christianity
were Jews. Luke records that some spoke Greek, including
converts to Judaism, such as Nicolas of Antioch, while others
presumably spoke Aramaic. Their growth was rapid and it
included a large number of Jewish priests who were converted
(Acts 6:1–7). Even the Ethiopian eunuch, an important official in
charge of his queen's treasury, had been in Jerusalem to worship
at the Temple (Acts 8:27,28). So in the early years, Christianity

was entirely a Jewish movement, and it caused some uproar when, after some ten or more years, it spread to the Gentiles. The apostle Peter was even called upon to explain himself (Acts 11:1–4,18). Hence the significance of the name 'Christian' being first used at Antioch around AD45 (Acts 11:26), for it was now no longer just a Jewish Messianic movement. This helps us importantly to appreciate the Jewish nature of the early church and to understand why Paul always started off his missionary visits in the synagogue before moving on the marketplace.

There is an important distinction to note here between Islam and Christianity. Islam started in Mecca, more than 650 miles from Jerusalem. It adopted many Jewish ideas, especially monotheism, and respected significant Judeo-Christian leaders, but it wasn't a Jewish movement. It started a long way away and its founder members were Arabs. As a consequence, it has a very different character.

Christianity, on the other hand, was fundamentally Jewish. From the outset, it sat under the authority of the Jewish Scriptures, and owned its patriarchs and prophets. It saw Jesus as the long-promised Jewish Messiah. It started among the Jews and remained an entirely Jewish movement for ten to fifteen years. So it is quite wrong then to think of 'The Church' as a separate, non-Jewish institution, which moved in to cherry-pick Jewish ideas to create a new religion. This becomes a serious and inflammatory error, when it is claimed that the New Testament Christians were being racist in accusing the Jews of killing Christ. Those first Christians were themselves Jews. Christ is a divisive figure in demanding ultimate allegiance (see Matt 10:34-39). But these divisions occurred within Jewish families and households, and still do. Some followed Jesus, believing him to be their promised Messiah and others opposed him vigorously. Listen to Luke's account:

Now those who were scattered, because of the persecution that arose over Stephen, travelled as far as Phoenicia and Cyprus and Antioch, speaking the word to no one except Jews. But there were some of them … who on coming to Antioch spoke to the [Greeks] also, preaching the Lord Jesus. And the hand of the Lord was with them, and a great number who believed turned to the Lord. The report of this came to the ears of the church in Jerusalem, and they sent Barnabas to Antioch...And a great many people were added to the Lord...For a whole year they met with the church and taught a great many people. And in Antioch the disciples were first called Christians.
(Acts 11:19–26)

So by AD49, when the Jews were expelled from Rome by Claudius, the Christians were only just establishing a distinctive identity. They had previously been seen as a troublesome Jewish sect. And if there were Christians in Pompeii twenty years later, they would most likely have also been predominantly Jewish, and in all probability had been expelled from Rome by Claudius. This explains the doorpost! The Jews had a long tradition of marking their faith on their doorposts. This went back 1,500 years to their exodus from Egypt (Exodus 12:7), when they were ordered to put the blood of the Passover lamb on their doorframes to assure them of divine protection. Annually until AD70, Jews continued to celebrate the Passover in Jerusalem, sacrificing a lamb in the Temple precincts to remind them of their deliverance from slavery.

After their exodus from Egypt, the Israelites were instructed to post the Shema, the most important Jewish affirmation, on their doorframes, which they continue to do to this day:

Hear, O Israel: the LORD our God, the LORD is one. You shall love the LORD your God with all your heart and with all your soul and with all your might. And these words that I command you today shall be on your heart. You shall teach them diligently to your children, and shall talk of them when you sit in your house and when you walk by the way, and when you lie down, and when you rise. You shall bind them as a sign on your hand, and they shall be as frontlets between your eyes. You shall write them on the doorposts of your house and on your gates.
(Deuteronomy 6:4–9)

Fifty days after the Passover (implied by the name Pentecost), there was one of three compulsory Jewish pilgrimage festivals (Exodus 23:14-17), attended by huge numbers. Luke records the nationalities present at the one following Christ's crucifixion (probably AD30 or 33):

Now there were dwelling in Jerusalem Jews, devout men from every nation under heaven...Parthians and Medes and Elamites and residents of Mesopotamia, Judea and Cappadocia, Pontus and Asia, Phrygia and Pamphylia, Egypt and the parts of Libya belonging to Cyrene, and visitors from Rome both Jews and [converts to Judaism]; Cretans and Arabians ...
(Acts 2:5,9–11)

And this was the day when the apostle Peter gave his first public address preaching that '... this Jesus, delivered up according to the definite plan and foreknowledge of God, you crucified and killed by the hands of lawless men. God raised him up...and of that we all are witnesses...'.And so the church was born. Luke reports: 'So those who received his word were baptised, and there were added that day about three thousand souls' (Acts 2:14–41). For these earliest Jewish Christians, as John the Baptist had announced, Jesus was seen as 'the Lamb of God, who takes away the sin of the world!' (John1:29). The Messianic prophesies about his sacrificial death (e.g. Isaiah 53) had been fulfilled. The kingly rule of God, the 'kingdom of heaven', had arrived. Faith in the Messiah now marked out the new 'Israel of God' (Galatians 6:16). Jesus had predicted in tears that the Temple in Jerusalem would be completely destroyed 'because you did not recognise the time of God's coming to you' (Luke 19: 41–44NIV). This prophecy was fulfilled in AD70 and the Passover sacrifice, which had been of supreme importance to the Jews, celebrating their freedom from slavery, came to a dramatic end. For the Jews this was a cataclysmic event, but for the Jewish Christians, the Temple had fulfilled its purpose. There was no need for any further sacrifice. The Lamb of God had died 'once for all' (Hebrews 9:26–28) bringing them freedom from slavery to sin, and the Christian believers themselves became the holy places where the Spirit of God lived. As Paul wrote, 'For we are the temple of the living God; as God said, 'I will make my dwelling place among them and walk among them, and I will be their God, and they will be my people' (2 Corinthians 6:16). For a Jewish baker in Pompeii, to etch a reminder of Christ's sacrificial death on his doorframe was wholly appropriate.

Was the baker a Jewish Christian?

There is other evidence besides the square on the doorpost. Two stars of David were etched outside the baker's home in Via Vesuvio and a large cross was found centrally above their oven. (Other crosses have been found in the excavation. Sceptics say that one in Herculaneum could have been a bracket for a shelf, but as an expert in very bad 'do-it-yourself' I have learned that you need two brackets to do that job!)

The bakery cross

Literate, learned and evidently successful, the baker and his wife are presented in a fabulous picture, which was found in the reception room of their house. Believed to have been painted around AD65, they appear as equal partners in business and in life together. Interestingly, she is dressed modestly for that promiscuous city and, in a male-dominated world, she is positioned in the foreground.

Terracotta images of male genitals are found in many streets and houses in Pompeii as a kind of lucky charm, but one in the baker's house appears to have been plastered over!

While there is no suggestion in Acts that Paul visited Pompeii, it is quite possible that a senior person from the bakery of Pompeii met the Alexandrian grain ship as it arrived in Puteoli in order to collect their wheat after the winter. They presumably needed to secure the right quantity, arrange for its transfer and negotiate its price. (From the picture of the wife looking so efficient with her wooden tablet and stylus, I suspect she might have managed that herself!)

There was also a detailed picture in their house of the baker seemingly giving away bread. In both pictures, he is dressed in a bleached toga, suggesting he could have been a candidate for election as an '*aedile*'. His name, Terentius Neo, is assumed from an electoral notice which was painted on a wall in his house. If that is the case, in Erastus of Corinth and Terentius of Pompeii we seem to have two very early examples of Christians taking their social responsibilities seriously as citizens and benefactors, at significant personal cost.

CHAPTER 16
IN CAESAR'S HOUSEHOLD
———•———

Priscilla and Aquila

The names of this husband and wife team occur seven times in the New Testament. They are mentioned four times in Acts 18 as well as in three of Paul's letters – Romans 16:3,4, 1 Corinthians 16:19 and 2 Timothy 4:19 – while residing variously in Rome, Corinth and Ephesus. We know so little about them, but what we do know is compelling and fascinating.

Whether or not Terentius Neo and his wife were Jewish Christians, their dynamic contemporaries, Priscilla and Aquila, certainly were. They are always mentioned together, with both being named. It is never just 'Aquila and his wife'.

I know Christian married couples who work in different roles. I think of a pastor married to a judge, a sociologist married to an economist, a science teacher married to a doctor. They each have their own spheres of influence: they write in different publications, and I occasionally catch up with them in different conferences – but they are never together, except on social occasions. Yet Aquila and Priscilla are always together! We don't get the impression that one of them was the main player while the other had a supporting role. Sometimes he is named first, but more often, she is, which may well be significant. Like the baker's wife, she seems to be placed in the foreground.

Paul first met them in Corinth and they became his fellow-workers. They had recently arrived there from Italy following the expulsion of Jews from Rome in AD49 (Acts 18:2). Aquila we are told was a Jew but that was not the only thing he had in common with Paul – he was also a tentmaker. And so Paul stayed with them (Acts 18:2,3). The natural reading is that he was their house guest for eighteen months, as no other accommodation for him is mentioned before they sailed together to Ephesus (Acts 18:18).

The passage implies that they were already Christians when Paul met them, as their conversions to Christ are not mentioned. They are presented not as new converts but as mature and capable Christian workers, who no doubt benefited enormously from personal tuition while living with Paul. A couple of years later, we are told that the church in Ephesus was meeting in their home (1 Corinthians 16:19). There they took the formidable new Jewish convert Apollos from Alexandria under their pastoral wing, inviting him to their home for further instruction in Christian basics (Acts 18:24-26). He then went on to Corinth (Acts 19:1), where he 'vigorously refuted his Jewish opponents in public debate' (Acts 18:28), clearly having a major ministry there, as did both Peter and Paul (1Corinthians 1:12).

We are also told that somewhere along the line, this husband and wife team risked their lives to rescue Paul (Romans 16:4) but we are not told the circumstances.

My wife and I have a Visitors' Book, which we started when we married in 1971. We have just had it rebound as it was falling apart. It records the names, dates and comments of everyone who has stayed in our home over the years (or rather, all those who remembered to sign it!). A few stayed for long periods, and for some who did, it was not easy. Different temperaments, eating habits, schedules and different ways of relaxing can make prolonged hospitality a struggle. Yet Chappo, a bachelor like Paul, was a frequent guest in our home and we loved it. He was funny, thoughtful, practical and relaxed. He would work in the kitchen and volunteer to push the pram. He introduced our children to Kipling's *Just So Stories* and playfully nicknamed our baby son 'King Rat'. Every meal was an event. He even helped us to move house, and with all our helpers, we gathered together in the evening for a takeaway meal of fish and chips. None of them will forget our 'Chippo with Chappo'. He was a wonderful and very amusing guest.

The fact that Paul stayed with Priscilla and Aquila for so long and they remained so devoted to him, says a great deal about the personal character of Paul. This links well with the deeply moving account of Paul's departure from Ephesus, where he knelt on the shore and prayed with the elders. Paul had been reminding them that his work had provided not only for his own needs but also for the needs of his companions, adding a saying of Jesus that is not found in the Gospels: 'It is more blessed to give than to receive.' Luke records, 'There was much weeping on the part of all; they embraced Paul and kissed him, being sorrowful most of all because of the word he had spoken, that they would not see his face again. And they accompanied him to the ship.' You could not make it up. It was a very real and emotional moment in time and speaks volumes about Paul's character (Acts 20:34–38).

Subsequently, Priscilla and Aquila returned to Rome (Romans 16:3,4), probably after the death of Claudius in AD54, when the emperor's edict against the Jews would have lapsed. The last we hear of them, however, they are back in Ephesus! (2 Timothy 4:19). So between AD49–65, these early missionaries went from Rome to Corinth, Corinth to Ephesus, Ephesus to Rome and back to Ephesus, no doubt stopping in Corinth on both journeys, as it was directly on route, and there was no Corinthian canal in those days to enable them to sail on by. The sort of work they were doing in Ephesus and Corinth (providing hospitality, opening their home for church meetings and training individuals such as Apollos) they also did in Rome 'Greet also the church in their house' (Romans 16:4,5), and may well have been doing it prior to their expulsion in AD49.

F.F.Bruce comments that Priscilla, or Prisca – to use her more formal name as Paul does, may have been of a higher social standing than her husband, belonging to the gens Prisca, a noble Roman family. That would fit the picture we have of her well, and her home within the city of Rome could have been a major centre for the bourgeoning church, many of whom would be slaves or ex-slaves.

Given that Luke records that there were Jewish visitors from Rome who heard Peter preach on the Day of Pentecost, it is quite possible that some of those 3,000 people, who became Christians that day and were baptised, took the gospel back to Rome with them, long before any of the apostles arrived there. Paul appears to have been the first, arriving in AD60, unless Peter had visited Rome some fifteen years earlier. We shall consider that possibility later.

Did Paul meet Seneca?

In the light of the growth and vigour of the church in Rome, I have to wonder whether the Christians there had contact with the Stoic philosopher Seneca. This Roman philosopher and statesman was born in Cordoba in southern Spain about the same year as Jesus, and died in Rome about the same year as Paul. I read something about him that greatly surprised me. I have in the past spent some time thinking about the uniqueness of Christ's Golden Rule, and Seneca seemed to have had a particularly good grasp of it.

Now, there is much confusion about the Golden Rule. This key saying of Christ, which Jesus said 'sums up the Law and the Prophets' (Matthew 7:12), is commonly and erroneously attributed to Confucius. Recently in *The London Times*, a writer attributed Christ's words to Rabbi Hillel. What Hillel actually said was: 'Do not do to your fellow man what is hateful to you. This is the entire Law, all the rest is commentary.'[62] If that summarises the totality of ethics, it is a disastrously negative maxim! Confucius stated his reciprocal rule in a similar way: 'Do not do to others what you would not like yourself, so that it might go well with you.' Both were negative ethics, prohibitions about things you should not do, with Confucius adding the motive that it was for your own benefit.

Aristotle had a positive but very restricted version: 'We should behave towards friends as we would wish friends to behave towards us'.

Christ, however, gave the world a uniquely positive and selfless command that applies to friends, enemies, and the whole of life: 'In everything, do to others what you would have them do to you' (Matthew 7:21,NIV). I can find no truly equivalent version to that rule prior to Christ.[63] Now Seneca's version in his Moral Letters is in spirit much closer to Christ's. He wrote with reference to slaves that you should 'treat your inferiors as you would like to be treated by your superiors'.[64] In contrast, Hillel or Confucius might have said, 'Do not do to your slave what is hateful to you', which has very different implications.

Nero became emperor on the death of Claudius in AD54 at the tender age of sixteen years, and two key advisors were appointed to help him. Seneca was appointed his tutor, personal advisor and speech writer, while Sextus Burrus, as head of the Praetorian Guard, was his security advisor. 'Burrus and Seneca were essential agents in establishing the young heir on the throne... Burrus backed the new emperor with the sword, while Seneca did so with words.'[65]

Seneca had a very mixed press. Rumours linked him with the death of Claudius and also of Nero's mother, Agrippina. He was enormously rich and in calling-in a huge loan to Britain, precipitated the Iceni uprising under Boudicca. Finally, he was accused of being a conspirator in an unsuccessful assassination attempt on Nero! Was he a Bonhoeffer to Rome's Hitler? Being a moral philosopher in the court of a maniacal tyrant, he was certainly caught between a rock and a very hard place. 'Without the backing of Burrus and the Praetorian Guard, Seneca's position in Nero's court became very weak and very dangerous.'[66]

Despite all this, he was much appreciated by the early Christians, who presumably thought he did his best in appalling circumstances. Tertullian spoke of him as 'often our own'.[67] In the brutal world of the Roman Empire, his kindness was evident. 'How little it is not to injure him whom you ought to help. Great praise that a man should be kind to man! Are we to bid a man to lend a hand to the shipwrecked, point the way to a stranger, share bread with the hungry?'[68]

He wrote that 'God made the world because he is good... He therefore made everything the best possible.'[69] 'God is near you, with you, within you[70] ...Not one of us is without his fault[71]

...No one will be found who can acquit himself: and any man calling himself innocent has regard to the witness, not to his own conscience[72] ...a holy spirit sits within us, spectator of our evil and our good, and guardian[73] ... None is a good man without God'.[74] Stunning as that is, and coming from the man who apparently gave us the phrase, 'to err is human', Seneca wrote something even more surprising: 'We ought to choose some good man and always have him before our eyes that we may live as if he watched us, and do everything as if he saw'.[75] 'It is without doubt a good thing to have set a guard over oneself, to whom you may look, whom you may feel present in your thoughts'.[76]

Lightfoot concluded that 'the Christian parallels in Seneca's writings become more frequent as he advances in life', though his philosophical stance and his behaviour gave no indication that he actually became a Christian.[77] The French Reformer Simon Goulart observed that a pagan reading Seneca would conclude he was a Christian, but a Christian reading Seneca would conclude he was a pagan![78]

Did Seneca know about Christ?

None of Seneca's writings mentions Jesus. But is that the long and the short of it?

I was also surprised by his 'Christian' attitude to slavery (see Ephesians 6:9; Colossians 4:1; Philemon 15,16) and the importance he attached to kindness. But given his acknowledgment that 'None is a good man without God', I was very surprised about his spiritual need for a 'good man' given his belief that 'to err is human', as it calls into question whether any such person exists! It sounds to me that something of Christian teaching had certainly 'rubbed off' on him. Is it possible? I think it is.

Before Paul left Corinth with Priscilla and Aquila, the Jews had created another public disturbance, in which they captured Paul and brought him before the proconsul Gallio (Acts 18:12). Gallio was actually Seneca's older brother and he plays an important role in dating these events. It had been widely assumed that Luke's account of Gallio being 'proconsul of Achaia' was a fiction. There was no record of him holding that post and it was disputed that such a post even existed. All that changed in 1905 when an inscription was discovered in Delphi in the Roman province of Achaia. It reads:

> Tiberius Claudius Caesar Augustus…12th year of tribunician power, acclaimed emperor for the 26th time, father of the country, sends greetings…as my friend and proconsul L. Iunius Gallio recently reported to me …

As proconsuls were in post for one year only, this gives us precise information to say he was in post in AD51 and implies therefore that Paul arrived in Corinth c. AD50 as well as underling the difficulties in the ancient world of expressing precise dates![79] It is one of many important details which have vindicated Luke as a careful and reliable historian and has provided a fixed point in the New Testament timeline.

Given the public disturbances that had happened in Rome just two years previously, to say nothing of riots in Philippi, Thessalonica, Ephesus and the other places at that time documented by Luke, is it likely that Gallio would not have raised the matter with his brother in the years that followed? Gallio had, after all, dismissed the case against one of their principal ringleaders.

Seneca and Burrus both stayed in post until AD62. So when

Paul arrived in Rome (c.AD60) Seneca was in a very powerful position. Paul was under house arrest in Rome for a full two years during that period with open access for visitors 'and welcomed all who came to him' ... and they came in 'greater numbers' (Acts 28:23,30).

In his letter to the Philippians, written while imprisoned in Rome, Paul says, 'what has happened to me has really served to advance the gospel, so that it has become known throughout the whole imperial guard and to all the rest that my imprisonment is for Christ. And most of the brothers, having become confident in the Lord by my imprisonment, are much more bold to speak the word without fear.' (Philippians 1:12-14).

The 'whole imperial guard,' (the praetorium) could refer to a place but more probably refers to the soldiers themselves, under the command of Burrus.[80] They were a large body of elite troops. If Paul was under house arrest at this time, it suggests that changing guards were present day by day, as 'He lived there two whole years at his own expense, and welcome all who came to him, proclaiming the kingdom of God and teaching about the Lord Jesus Christ with all boldness and without hindrance.' (Acts 28:30,31).

But at the end of that letter he sent greetings 'especially [from] those of Caesar's household' (Philippians 4:22). Of course, this could have referred to slaves and menial servants. But that sounds very unlikely; why would he send their anonymous greetings to Philippi? The assumption has to be that people in Philippi would know whom he meant. If they were more prominent persons, given the turbulent history, would they not have wished to remain unidentified? Today, in writing to missionaries working discreetly in Muslim lands, we have to be careful what we say, so as not to blow away their cover. Surely Paul, in telling the

Philippians about his ministry at the heart of the empire, would need to be cautious. Nicodemus, that 'ruler of the Jews' famously came to see Jesus 'by night' (John 3:1). People in power need to be discreet.

Bishop Lightfoot wrote a fascinating paper on St Paul and Seneca, and in writing his commentary on Philippians thought to check out the personal names listed at the end of Romans, to see if any overlapped with known lists of members of Caesar's household at that time. He found more than a dozen! Of course, he could not be sure that any of them were the same people mentioned by Paul, but some of these names were rare, increasing that likelihood. He was certainly able to establish that names on Paul's list were current among names in Caesar's household at that time.[81]

Now I am not suggesting that Seneca or Burrus visited Paul personally during his house arrest. We do not know, but it was certainly possible. However, by his own account, Seneca made a practice of dining with his slaves and engaging them in familiar conversation.[82] If members of Caesar's household were visiting Paul, or were members of the Christian community in Rome, he could have learned about Jesus from them. But they would not have had their Bibles on the table! They may well have learned parts of the Sermon on the Mount, remembered some of the parables and have had a real grasp of the significance of Christ's claims, identity, death and resurrection. Philologus and Nereus, Tryphaena and Tryphosa were all found on Caesar's household list, as was the relatively rare name, Stachys. Did they introduce Seneca to Andronicus and Junias to hear their account of Christ's resurrection? If Prisca was from noble stock, I am sure she would not have missed a chance. Perhaps one of them even carried letters between Seneca and Paul, though no authentic letters have survived. 'The legend is not without a certain plausibility' concludes classical scholar, Emily Wilson.[83] Eventually Seneca, implicated in a conspiracy against Nero, was forced to commit suicide in AD65.

Importantly, the gospel in Rome was being spread by word of mouth and lived out in the lives of Christian people long before Paul's arrival. With the Jews, Paul tried to convince them about Jesus from the Law of Moses and from the Prophets. To everyone, he proclaimed the kingdom of God and taught them 'about the Lord Jesus Christ' (Acts 28:23,31). They in turn became Christ's own persuasive documents, 'You yourselves are our letter of recommendation from Christ to be known and read by all,' as Paul delightfully put it. 'You are letter from Christ delivered by us, written not with ink but with the Spirit of the living God, not on tablets of stone but on tablets of human hearts' (2 Corinthians 3:2,3).

A recent survey in my local Southampton University showed that the commonest objection to Christianity was that students did not believe that Jesus ever existed! Not only would that mean that the finest and most remarkable figure in all history was pure invention, but so were his memorable sayings, his moral teaching, his Golden Rule, the Beatitudes, the Sermon on the Mount, the Lord's Prayer, his parables, his acts of compassion and his execution under Pontius Pilate. As Rousseau observed, 'The Gospel has marks of truth so great, so striking, so perfectly inimitable, that the inventor of it would be more astonishing than the hero.'[84]

More than that, the explosive growth of the early church has to be explained. It didn't suddenly arise out of hot air, nor did it evolve slowly over several generations. The facts are that in the first century, Jesus took the world by storm. As New Testament scholar Professor Charlie Moule once put it: 'You have to find a launching pad to launch this missile.'

CHAPTER 17
THE DISAPPEARANCE OF PETER

———·———

There is much we would like to know about the first twenty-five years of the Christian era. The New Testament tells us only part of the story, and we have been looking at some of the clues which help to paint the wider picture as to how it happened. We have looked at their manner of life, their energy in their travel, their central convictions, their hospitality, their relentless enthusiasm even in the teeth of violent persecution. And all this without a Bible between them!

Let us return now to the mysterious disappearance of their leading apostle.

His name appears some eighty times in the Gospels, and each Gospel records that he was originally called Simon, but Jesus gave him a new name, Peter (Cephas in Aramaic) meaning a rock (e.g. John 1:40–42).

Peter plays the lead role in the early narrative of Acts. He was the chief spokesman when the church was born at Pentecost (Acts 1,2), he preached powerfully in the Temple portico (Acts

3), he addressed the Jewish Council (Acts 4) and exposed the corruption of Ananias and Sapphira (Acts 5). When Samaritans became Christians, Peter and John were sent to investigate (Acts 8). Peter was travelling 'here and there among them all' building up the church in 'all Judea and Galilee and Samaria' (Acts 9:31,32) and he was the first to preach to the Gentiles some ten or more years after the birth of the church, albeit to a private audience in Caesarea (Acts 10:34–44).

Around AD42-44, another leading apostle, James, the brother of John, was executed by Herod Agrippa, grandson of Herod the Great, and Peter was also arrested (Acts 12:1–5). After the Passover, Peter, bound in chains between two soldiers with sentries at the door, was rescued from prison in quite remarkable circumstances and went directly to the home of the mother of John Mark (more of him shortly). When Peter appeared at their door, they couldn't believe it! They were amazed at his escape: 'But motioning to them with his hand to be silent, he described to them how the Lord had brought him out of the prison. And he said, "Tell these things to James [the brother of Jesus] and to the brothers." Then he departed and went to another place' (Acts 12:6–19).

There is no further record of Peter for some five years! Eventually, he would reappear in the Acts narrative at the Council of Jerusalem in c.AD49/50.

His arrest was no small matter. 'When [Herod] had seized him, he put him in prison, delivering him over to four squads of soldiers to guard him...Now when day came, there was no little disturbance among the soldiers over what had become of Peter. And after Herod had searched for him and did not find him, he examined the sentries and ordered that they should be put to death' (Acts 12:4,18,19). Herod himself died shortly afterwards, Luke's record of his death being confirmed by the Jewish historian Josephus.[86]

So what happened to Peter over the next five years? Luke's short sentence, 'he departed and went to another place' (Acts 12:17) is, I think, pregnant with meaning. He evidently 'departed', so we can assume he did not stay in Jerusalem. Neither did he move from hiding place to hiding place like a fugitive. Luke seems emphatic that he went to a specific location, and that would have to be outside Palestine if the phrase 'another place', means, as seems probable, 'a place beyond Herod's jurisdiction'. If Luke knew that 'place', and the specificity of the phrase suggests to me that he did, why did he not say where it was?

One might immediately think that he was trying to protect Peter, until you realise that Luke's account was written over twenty years later. Did he therefore not want to jeopardise Peter in Rome by pointing out that he was an escaped prisoner? Peter, it seems, was there during the persecution of Nero, and Luke was also there at that time (2 Timothy 4:11). So he effectively writes that Peter was the name of a notorious leader in Jerusalem some twenty years ago. End of message.

I have suggested that Peter could have arrived in Rome fifteen years before Paul did. The possibility here is that, pursued by Herod, he escaped from Jerusalem under the cover of a large exodus of Passover pilgrims returning to Rome. It is impossible to imagine that Peter, like a rabbit on the run, quietly 'went to ground'. We know that before AD54 he had a ministry in Corinth (1 Corinthians 1:12) and apparently took his wife with him (1 Corinthians 9:5, see also Matthew 8:14). And we can assume that Peter was not in Rome in AD57, as Paul makes no mention of him in his letter to Rome that year, when sending greetings to some thirty other, named individuals. (Romans 16:3–16).

The early church had clearly understood that Peter founded the church in Rome, and the tradition that he was martyred there around AD65–67 goes unchallenged to this day. (If so, Luke's silence, it seems, did not protect him from the madness of Nero!) It is interesting, then, to read Peter and Paul's views of each other's work. The Jerusalem council was brought about because of the Gentile mission, and the main question before them was whether Gentiles should be circumcised. By Luke's account, after there had been much debate on the subject (can't you just imagine it?), Peter spoke powerfully in support of the rightness of Paul's mission to the Gentiles: 'Brothers, you know that in the early days God made a choice among you, that by my mouth the Gentiles should hear the word of the gospel and believe. And God, who knows the heart, bore witness to them, by giving them the Holy Spirit just as he did to us, and he made no distinction between us and them... why are you putting God to the test by placing a yoke on the neck of the disciples…?' (Acts 15:7–10).

Paul comments in an early letter about Peter: '… when [the influential leaders] saw that I had been entrusted with the gospel to the uncircumcised, just as Peter had been entrusted with the gospel to the circumcised (for he who worked through Peter for his apostolic ministry to the circumcised worked also through me for mine to the Gentiles), and when James and [Peter] and John, who seemed to be pillars, perceived the grace that was given to me, they gave the right hand of fellowship to Barnabas and me, that we should go to the Gentiles and they to the circumcised' (Galatians 2:7–9).

This suggests they were both reporting back, having been busy in their separate and equally important but distinct spheres. The date of this meeting is unclear. Paul records that it happened 'after fourteen years' (Galatians 2:1) but is unclear whether this counts from his Damascus road experience or from his visit to Peter and James in Jerusalem three years later. It is probable that the first meeting was in the mid AD30s and the second in the late AD40s. Anyway, it is clear that Paul and Peter mutually respected each other's work, implying that they saw each other as the two principle leaders of the Christian mission. Neither had the primacy, as is evident by Paul correctly rebuking Peter for his yielding to pressure from the Jews to stop eating with Gentiles in Antioch (Galatians 2:11–14).

Whether or not Peter went to Rome early on, Paul states his own reason for not going to Rome: 'I make it my ambition to preach the gospel, not where Christ has already been named, lest I build on someone else's foundation...This is the reason why I have so often been hindered from coming to you. But now...I hope to see you in passing as I go to Spain, and to be helped on my journey there by you, once I have enjoyed your company for a while' (Romans 15:20–24).

We know there was a very large community of Jews in Rome. Many of their ancestors had been taken there as slaves 100 years previously, after the Roman army under Pompey the Great had conquered Judea in 63BC. We have three good reasons to think there was a vigorous Christian movement growing among them. Firstly, the 'Jews' were expelled from Rome in AD49 under Claudius 'on account of a dispute over Chrestus'.[87] Secondly, Paul refused to visit Rome earlier, so as not to build on another apostle's foundation. Thirdly, because Paul was able to say, just eight years later and entirely without his help: 'I thank my God through Jesus Christ for all of you, because your faith is being reported all over the world' (Romans 1:8).

What did he mean by 'all over the world'? Well, it certainly meant the Mediterranean world, if not the entire Roman Empire and beyond. Felix was governor of Judea from AD52–58 when Paul appeared before him in AD57. His accuser, Tertullus, said: 'We have found this man a plague, one who stirs up riots among all the Jews throughout the world and is a ringleader of the sect of the Nazarenes'(Acts 24:5). A similar charge was made in AD49 in Thessalonica: 'These men who have caused trouble all over the world have now come here...They are all defying Caesar's decrees, saying that there is another king, one called Jesus.' (Acts 17:6,7 NIV)

An executed criminal was being widely promoted as a rival to the emperor! The deceased Emperor Augustus had been hailed as both lord and god, the saviour of the world and the bringer of peace and justice. Those Jews who rejected Christ as their Messiah certainly knew how to press the right political buttons to provoke trouble.

At the beginning of his reign, Claudius wrote to the people of Alexandria in AD41:

'Do not bring in or invite Jews who sail to Alexandria from Syria or from other parts of Egypt; this will make me suspect you the more, and I will impose severe penalties on them for fomenting a general plague throughout the whole world.'[88]

Whether the concern here was about Jewish zealots or a rival king called Jesus is unclear, but it needs to be remembered that following the martyrdom of Stephen,

'... there arose on that day a great persecution against the church in Jerusalem, and they were all scattered throughout the regions of Judea and Samaria, except the apostles' (Acts 8:1). This happened at a very early stage, before Paul had even left for Damascus.

Apollos was a Jewish native of Alexandria, where there was a significant Jewish population. It seems he was already a Christian when he arrived in Ephesus (Acts 18:24f). John Mark himself is said to have died in Alexandria, having travelled there from Rome. The key points are that travel around the Mediterranean was easy for six months of the year and trade between seaports was very busy. And the emperor was already anxious about Jewish revolts in the year he came to power.

So, who laid that Christian foundation among the Jews in Rome, which would be reported 'all over the world', if not Peter? When Paul talks here about a 'foundation', he has to mean an apostolic foundation. This was not just 'wild fruit' whose seeds were blown by the wind and were flourishing spontaneously. That would certainly have encouraged Paul to go to Rome to lay a good foundation himself. Rather, this must have been the fruit of apostolic work, and Paul was being particularly anxious to work effectively alongside but not in competition with any other apostle (a lesson learned from Corinth, perhaps?).

If Peter, the apostle to the Jews, laid the foundations for the church in Rome in that large Jewish community during the AD40s, it is clear that by the time Paul wrote to them in AD57, there was now a growing Gentile community among them.

If the general drift of this is true, it leads to another major possibility. Enter John Mark. Peter had escaped to Mark's mother's home in Jerusalem, where we are told that many were gathered together in prayer. Mark's home had evidently become a Christian centre at a time of crisis. Mark first appears in Luke's narrative with Barnabas and Paul on their return (to Antioch?) from Jerusalem, where they had been delivering famine relief (Acts 12:25). He then went with them to Cyprus (Acts 13:4,5) but returned to Jerusalem, leaving Paul in Perga in Pamphylia (in what is now southern Turkey). Barnabas and Paul later fell out over this. Barnabas wanted his cousin Mark to join them on a return trip, but Paul resisted this as Mark had previously deserted them (Acts 15:36–39). It seems, however, that Paul later forgave him (Colossians 4:10; Philemon 24). It is clear from Paul's letter to the Colossians that Mark was then with Paul in Rome around AD62 (but there is still no mention of Peter being there).

However, Peter's first letter, generally dated to have been written around AD62/63 from Rome (referred to as 'Babylon') also acknowledges the presence of 'Mark, my son', who sends his greetings (1Peter 5:13). Yet Mark was not there when Paul wrote his second letter to Timothy near the end of his life c.AD64/67: 'Luke alone is with me. Get Mark and bring him with you, for he is very useful to me for ministry' (2 Timothy 4:11). It seems from this that Mark must have been helping Timothy in Ephesus.

Bishop Papias was a church leader around AD100. His writings were known to Iranaeus, who described Papias as 'a hearer of John and companion of Polycarp'.[89] Papias is quoted by the historian Eusebius, who claimed he was quoting him directly in this passage:

The Elder [John?] used to say this also: Mark became the interpreter of Peter, and he wrote down accurately, though not in order, as much as he remembered of the sayings and doings of Christ. For he was not a hearer or a follower of the Lord, but afterwards, as I said, of Peter, who adapted his teachings to the needs of the moment and did not make an ordered exposition of the sayings of the Lord. And so Mark made no mistake when he thus wrote down some things as he [Peter] remembered them; for he made it his especial care to omit nothing of what he heard and to make no false statement therein.[90]

The need to interpret Peter may have been in the translation of

Peter's teaching from Aramaic or from poor Greek into better Greek. Papias also made the claim that Matthew's Gospel was originally drafted in Hebrew.

So this tradition about Mark recording Peter's teaching seems to have been accepted at the end of the first century and reaches back into living memory.[91] Internal evidences linking Mark with Peter include the similarities with the structure of Peter's speech in Acts 10:34–43, the way he makes no attempt to hide Peter's blushes in describing his weaknesses and in the way he avoided giving him praise.

Dating the Gospels has always been difficult. Over the past fifty years, a date for Mark's Gospel of around AD60 has held by a broad consensus. It is disputed whether Mark depended on Matthew or Matthew on Mark, and no record of an original Hebrew text for Matthew has ever been discovered.

Yet it is generally agreed that Luke anyway was dependent on Mark's material for his Gospel, which in turn was presumably written before Luke wrote Acts. But Acts only takes us up to about AD62 and does not mention the deaths of Peter or Paul around AD64-67, while it does report the earlier martyrdoms of Stephen and James. Neither does he mention Nero setting fire to the Christians in Rome in AD64, an event which may be alluded to in Peter's first letter in his reference to faith 'tested by fire' (1Peter 1:7). These all suggest a pre-AD64 date for Acts, an earlier date for Luke's Gospel, and therefore an even earlier one for Mark. (See Appendix 1)

On this basis, Mark's Gospel could not be a record of Peter's teaching in Rome after AD62, and Peter does not appear to have been in Rome in AD57, while in the early AD50s, Jews were clearly not welcome there at all! Had Peter sneaked into Rome then, he would have been evangelising Gentiles, which he did not see as his job. So there was not a lot of scope for Mark recording Peter's teaching in Rome during the AD50 or 60s. In fact, the New Testament surprisingly makes no overt mention of Peter going to Rome at all!

However, we started by noting that when Peter escaped from prison, he went directly to the home of Mark's mother in Jerusalem. Why did he go there? If Mark was a valued assistant for Paul and Barnabas in Cyprus in AD46 (Acts 12:25; 13:5, 2Timothy 4:11), he may also have been working with Peter in his early ministry in Judea, Galilee and Samaria (Acts 9:31). If Paul was to teach about Jesus, whom he had never directly heard, he would have needed Mark's records of Peter's early preaching and eyewitness testimony.

The church historian Eusebius, writing around AD340, said Peter arrived in Rome in the early years of the reign of the Emperor Claudius (AD41–54). The silence in the New Testament about Peter's arrival in Rome seems to present us with a choice. Mark either recorded Peter's teaching wherever they travelled together in the AD50s, or he started writing it in Rome before the expulsion of the Jews in AD49.

I am assuming that the substantial work done in Rome was not achieved by fleeting apostolic visits. Laying good foundations takes time. Neither should we assume that any of the Gospels suddenly appeared overnight, even though earlier drafts have not survived. Writing doesn't work like that. Some of my ideas in this book were originally published back in 1990,[92] much it of it has appeared in website articles[93] and in a monthly newsletter over several years.[94] The remaining sections and the final editing were done in 2015. It is probable that Mark, who did not have the luxury of any 'cut and paste' primitive word processor, worked on his writing project over an extended period. His records may well have assisted Paul and Barnabas in Cyprus and were almost certainly known to Luke (Luke 1:1) even if his work was finally completed and made public in Rome. When written material is gathered together in a completed work, the earlier drafts are then liable to be ignored and forgotten.

This leaves us with these distinct and fascinating possibilities:

- that Peter laid the foundations of the church in Rome between AD 44–49;
- that Peter's preaching caused uproar among the Jews in Rome, as it had done in Jerusalem (Acts 4:2–4);
- that John Mark wrote it down, in whole or in part, either earlier or later, in Judea or in Rome, and
- that publishing it, in whole or in part, precipitated the riots in Rome;
- that Claudius thought he would resolve this turmoil by expelling the whole Jewish community from Rome in AD49, with the result that they were scattered all over the known world, with some of them anyway carrying drafts of Mark's Gospel in their luggage! If so, Claudius had made a big miscalculation.

So that is my layman's take on it, but I am pleased to find a good number of New Testament scholars are in agreement with some, anyway, of my central conclusions. So John Robinson, who argued that the entire New Testament was written before the destruction of the Temple in Jerusalem in AD70,[95] wrote that 'the first draft of Mark's Gospel could be as early as 45'.[96] James Crossley, in his doctoral thesis, based on internal evidence of the Jewishness of the gospel, concludes that Mark was likely to have been written between AD35 and 45.[97] Paul Barnett has written, 'There is no reason in principle that Mark could not have been written in Caesarea Maritima sometime in the 50s.'[98] I was delighted to find that in 1972 John Wenham had put forward a similar theory of Peter escaping to Rome but it seems to have been largely ignored.[99]

I have suggested a Time Line in Appendix 1. There is room for flexibility but I can't imagine that any of those dates will be far out in. There are some known unknowns, such as the actual year of Christ's death and resurrection, the year Paul met Peter and James in Jerusalem or the year the gospel was first preached to the Gentiles. But there is not a lot of room for manoeuvre in any of this, as I hope this study has shown. Many pieces of this jigsaw puzzle slot easily together and Acts has been vindicated time and again as being a very careful piece of historical work. The wholesale dismissal of the authenticity of the New Testament documents that I heard recently from a leading Humanist spokesperson at the 2015 European Skeptics Conference in London was clearly not sceptical enough. It was blinded by prejudice and seriously ill-informed.

In the twenty-first century after seventy years, Holocaust deniers are still being silenced by the living memory of eyewitnesses or the close relatives of those eyewitnesses. So in the first century, the eye witnesses played the crucial role. Richard Bauckham is satisfied that 'Mark's Gospel was written well within the lifetime of many of the eyewitnesses'.[100] His central argument is that 'the period between the "historical" Jesus and the Gospels was spanned...by the continuing presence and testimony of the eyewitnesses, who remained the authoritative sources of their traditions until their deaths'. So, the key factor informing and controlling the Gospel writers, was not so much the dates of the earliest written texts nor the oral traditions that had been passed on by memory, but the living testimony of the eyewitnesses themselves.[101]

CHAPTER 18
THE FUTURE FOR CHRISTIANITY

——•——

What does the future hold for Christianity? In much of Europe, it is currently losing ground dramatically. The media see us as being on the 'wrong side of history'. Yet in the past fifty years we have witnessed some enormous developments, which must shape the next fifty years. I believe they give us solid grounds for encouragement.

1) The historicity of the New Testament

From the beginning of my personal search, I wanted to know what critical scholars made of the authenticity of the foundational New Testament documents, and one of the books I bought was *The Rise of Christianity* by E.W. Barnes, published in 1947. Barnes was the Bishop of Birmingham and a radical thinker. So I was surprised to find that he actually accepted that the apostle Paul was the original author of the first Letter to the Corinthians and that he also accepted the dating, which is generally agreed today, that it was written in or about AD54, some twenty to twenty-five years after Christ's crucifixion.

The trouble was that he thought much of the contents of that letter were added in later, particularly chapter 15, which he placed in the second century![102] This chapter deals with the evidence for the resurrection. His thesis was that this was a very late addition, implying that it had evolved as an idea over the previous 100 years. This, of course, would lay an axe to the root of Christian belief, and many people felt that the bishop should, at least, have resigned his living.

That the resurrection of Christ was pivotal to the Christian story was becoming increasingly evident to me as I wrestled with these documents. So, I asked myself, was it there from the beginning – the driving force that propelled the gospel across the Roman Empire and deeply into three continents within a generation, or was it an attractive myth that evolved gradually over 100 years but had no basis in historical reality?

Within twenty-five years of Barnes' book, the eminent Cambridge New Testament scholar C.H.Dodd published *The Founder of Christianity*. The climax of it was his important treatment of 1 Corinthians 15. He was, it seems, the first scholar to publish at a popular level the idea that the little credal statement in verses 3 to 5 is historically 'the earliest known recital of the facts', which take us back 'a long way behind the gospels'.[103] Written in a structured, rhythmic format to aid memory for oral transmission, indicated by the technical Greek words used in its first sentence, the passage reads, (adding hyphens to highlight the rhythmic structure):

What I received, I passed on to you as of first importance:
that Christ died – for our sins – according to the Scriptures –
and was buried

and was raised – on the third day – according to the Scriptures
– and appeared
to Cephas and to the Twelve.

Paul then listed other resurrection appearances– to James, to all
the apostles and 'to more than five hundred of the brothers and
sisters at the same time, most of whom are still living, though
some have fallen asleep' (1 Corinthians 15:6 NIV), and lastly
to Paul himself. But the only two individuals he actually names
are Cephas (Aramaic for Peter) and James. Paul was clear that
he did not invent this fixed oral tradition which was 'of first
importance'(1 Corinthians 15:3). He said it was passed on to him
by others.

So, when did Paul memorise this creed, and who taught it
to him? He could have received it initially after his conversion,
when he first arrived in Damascus. But Dodd maintained that it
was anyway no later than the time of his meeting in Jerusalem
some three years later, when he was able to interrogate those
he named, the apostles Peter and James, the Lord's brother,
who became the leader of the Jerusalem church. Paul described
this meeting in his letter to the Galatians, where he recorded
that three years after his Damascus Road experience, he visited
Jerusalem and stayed with Peter for fifteen days, and he also met
James the Lord's brother. Crucially, Paul put himself on oath for
these statements: 'In what I am writing to you, before God, I do
not lie!' (Galatians 1:18-20)[104]

Dodd's arguments have become pivotal in New Testament
scholarship. This credal statement that Barnes had dated to the
second century, Dodd now traced on purely historical grounds
to 'almost certainly not more than seven years, possibly no more
than four' from the events themselves.[105]

Today, some, such as Gary Habermas, would place it even earlier.[106] There is dispute about the year Christ died. If it was in the spring of AD30, Paul could have been heading for Damascus that autumn and returning to Jerusalem to meet Peter and James in AD33. Furthermore, the phrase 'after three years' could also mean 'in the third year', shortening the time span further.

Presumably Paul was not the first to memorise this creed, which had been formulated in the interim, having grown out of the apostles' reflections on the meaning of Christ's death and his post-resurrection appearances. Far from evolving slowly with time, these central truths can be traced back on firm historical grounds to the very earliest years of the Christian era.

Dodd's book illustrates the revolution that has occurred in the past fifty years as to what we now know about the integrity of the NT documents, and it is very difficult to imagine that, as a collection of writings, they could ever be substantially undermined again.

2) The world religions

It was in 1968 that the Beatles went to India. There were, of course, many Indian immigrants in Britain at that time, but they tended to live in isolated communities. They largely kept themselves to themselves and most English people knew very little about them. 'This sceptred isle ... This fortress built by Nature', as Shakespeare put it,[107] was very self-contained and inward-looking. The newspaper headline of October 1957, 'Heavy Fog in Channel – Continent Cut Off' captured our view that we 'little Englanders' were at the centre of the world, and religion at the world's centre was nominally Christian for almost everyone.

The Beatles in going to India introduced us, with an enormous amount of publicity beamed into our homes, to the exotic and colourful world of other religions. Gurus like Maharishi Mahesh Yogi, with their ashrams, telling of ancient mysteries, teaching transcendental meditation and cosmic consciousness, wearing garlands of flowers and making invocations of love and peace, were accompanied by the fabulous and previously unheard music of Ravi Shankar on his sitar.

This was a far cry from the formal, dull rituals of the Church of England, with its Victorian hymns and ponderous organ music. Of course, the trip ended in tears and recriminations for the Beatles. The Maharishi admitted he was 'only human' and seemed to them more interested in females, fame and fortune than the deeper matters of the soul. Lennon's marriage broke up in the wake of it and the Beatles found drugs to be more enlightening than meditation.

Today, there is a huge amount of literature on the world's religions, but their mystique has very largely faded. Their histories and ideas are now readily available to us. It is now generally conceded that the Eastern pantheistic religions could never have given rise to science, or to the Protestant Work Ethic – or indeed, the Western civilisation, which has resulted from them both. There is now no possibility of a wonderful, ancient creed rescuing modern humanity from its problems. Furthermore, none of these other ancient religious systems readily cross cultures. Christianity alone has freely taken root around the world, and is now owned in every continent and within every major culture.

I remember my astonishment hearing the BBC news announcing some thirty years ago that 'Christian Revival has broken out in Outer Mongolia'. In South Korea, which was also traditionally Buddhist, Christianity has grown dramatically since World War Two and has played a major role in the modernisation of the country. Today they export as many missionaries as the United States. When I was at medical school, we prayed regularly for China, but Mao Tse-tung was in power. No news was coming out and we feared the worst for any surviving Christian students. But now, Bibles are being printed in China as fast as the machines can produce them, and there has been a massive turning to Christ. Protestant churches are growing rapidly, both in the official church and in the underground church. They are also growing at a dramatic rate in South America, Africa and across Asia. Islamic countries can only compete by banning Bibles and preventing the preaching of Christ by threats of appalling violence, but in these days of global travel and internet communications, their attempts at thought control are increasingly inadequate.

3) Welfare and human rights

Why is Christianity making such an impact around the world? On a visit to Uganda, I found the grave in Kampala of medical missionary and research pioneer Dr Albert Cook MD. Born in 1870, he responded as a newly qualified doctor to the call of the explorer Henry Morton Stanley to give his professional life to the service of Christ for the Ugandan people. Cook arrived there in 1897. The causes of tropical diseases were then largely unknown and became the focus of his research, for which he was awarded a doctorate. He was subsequently given a knighthood for his services to medicine. He died in Kampala aged eighty-one. When I returned home from my visit, I told a medical friend about him, knowing that he had been brought up by missionaries in Uganda. 'Oh yes, I visited him as a child,' Tim replied, 'and my father wrote an account of his life in the *British Medical Journal*.'[108] We were just two lifetimes away from the beginning of research into tropical medicine.

In a nearby grave was pioneer missionary James Hannington, the first Bishop of Eastern Equatorial Africa who was martyred in 1885 before ever reaching Kampala. Another grave belonged to a pioneer educationalist. Teaching people to read and write has been a particular concern for Christians, so that everyone can learn about Jesus for themselves. So literacy has been a major by-product of global mission.

There I was in Uganda visiting my son-in-law, who was promoting pioneer 'justice for the poor' work among Ugandan lawyers. Medicine, education, justice and the rule of law are major areas where Christians have made a massive contribution to the welfare of humanity across the world. Other major fields include the spread of stable democracy, human rights, prison reform, the care of children, the dignity of women and the liberation of slaves.

Let us briefly take just one example from this list, which is close to my heart. I have four children and so far, have thirteen grandchildren, so I spend a lot of time with these little ones. Consider how Christ's teaching has revolutionised attitudes to children all over the world. Today we just assume these are 'normal' human values, as though they arrived automatically in our mother's milk. Yet before 1833, little children in Britain were forced to work in industry. The Factory Act, championed by Christ-inspired Lord Shaftesbury, started a revolution. It banned children under nine from working in factories, while children aged thirteen to eighteen were then limited to working no more than twelve hours a day! Previously they were treated in Britain like slaves; now they were to commence two hours of schooling each day. Nothing empowers children more than education. We easily forget how recent this was and what drove these changes.

'Now they were bringing even infants to him that he might touch them. And when the disciples saw it, they rebuked them. But Jesus called them to them, saying, "Let the children come to me and do not hinder them, for to such belongs the kingdom of God. Truly, I say to you, whoever does not receive the kingdom like a child shall not enter it" (Luke 18:15-17).

'Whoever humbles himself like this child is the greatest in the kingdom of heaven.' (Matthew 18:4).

'And he sat down and called the twelve. And he said to them, "If anyone would be first, he must be last of all and servant of all." And he took a child and put him in the midst of them, and taking him in his arms, he said to them, "Whoever receives one such child in my name receives me, and whoever receives me, receives not me but him who sent me" (Mark 9:35–37). In other words, the child is an ambassador and representative of God himself.

Or consider this, reported in Matthew, Mark and Luke: 'whoever causes one of these little ones who believe in me to sin, it would be better for him to have a great millstone fastened around his neck and to be drowned in the depth of the sea' (Matthew 18:6). That is unsubtle, isn't it? The sins committed against children damage them for life, making them all the more likely to repeat them in their turn, so the sins of the parents echo down the generations. Jesus repeatedly talked about children and said they should be treated with the utmost love, care and respect. They are deeply precious in God's sight. And yet needy, vulnerable, uneducated children are being abused all over the world.

4) Moral values

The invention of the contraceptive pill raised enormous questions about personal morality. Where do moral and social obligations and duties come from? The history of humanity has harboured the view that ultimate values are 'givens' and not inventions. They belong to the absolute nature of things. The ancient Greeks attributed them to the gods. The ancient East attributed them to a different pantheon of gods. Though individuals down the centuries may have been atheists, the world population at large, in every culture and tribe, has been almost universally religious, if Buddhism counts as a religion.

It was only in the nineteenth century that the idea of atheism was pressed upon popular imagination. Famously, Nietzsche put these words into the mouth of a madman: '"Whither is God?" he cried. "I shall tell you. We have killed him – you and I. All of us are his murderers. God is dead and we have killed him. How shall we, the murderers of all murderers, comfort ourselves?"'[109]

An immediate impact of this is moral. Dostoyevsky observed that 'Without God, everything is permissible'. Why? Because there will be no recompense: we would be accountable to no one. There would be no objective moral values, no moral laws and no ultimate justice. Without God there is no basis for moral obligation or duty. We are all free agents, like animals in the jungle, following our own desires. And adultery, rape, theft, deception and murder are not things that mere animals worry about.

Nietzsche's human-centred philosophy was profoundly influential on Hitler. For me in the 1960s, atheism impacted my soul by reading the novels of the French Existentialists. They stared into the bleakness of a truly amoral world.

But deep in the human psyche we are all aware of evil: evil desires in ourselves, evil choices before us and evil deeds around us. We might disagree as to what constitutes evil, but the torturing of children for pleasure or the atrocities of Boko Haram or ISIS would settle the matter for most us. Evil exists.

So philosopher William Lane Craig formulates the argument: 'If God does not exist, objective moral values do not exist. But [surely], objective moral values do exist, therefore God exists.' Without God, there cannot be any objective, transcendent reality of either good or evil. Life would then be intrinsically non-moral. The very existence of evil is not, after all, an argument against the existence of God, but for him.[110]

This objection that people cannot believe in God because of the evil in the world now takes on a whole new perspective. It is only meaningful to talk about evil if God exists. If he does not exist, then neither good nor evil ultimately exist either. All we are left with are the harsh realities of life, along with our personal and social preferences. 'We would sooner not be tortured, raped or killed, because we don't like it.' But if God does not exist, we can hardly discuss such behaviour in terms of moral obligations or duties.

The Christian works on the assumption that God does exist and that good and evil are ultimate realities, so it really does matter how we behave. That is why Christ spent his time on earth 'doing good and healing all who were oppressed by the devil, for God was with him' (Acts 10:38).And all those who follow Christ believe we are not mere animals but are created in the likeness of God. We are therefore called to invest our days doing good and opposing evil. The crucifixion of Christ is evidence enough that evil exists and the resurrection of Christ is the great sign for the world that evil will ultimately be overcome.

5) The origins of the universe

In the 1960s there was relentless public debate about the origins of the universe. The ancient idea that the universe had an infinite past was championed by Cambridge astronomer Professor Fred Hoyle. He maintained the universe existed in a 'steady state'. How he held this view in the light of the Second Law of Thermodynamics I still don't understand, because that law expresses what we all know: that fires go out, that heat dissipates and that warm houses get cold unless you keep burning more fuel. Yet that is what he and many others believed about the universe, that it was eternal and would somehow avoid heat death.

Offering a different perspective had been astronomer Edwin Hubble. In the 1920s, he observed that the universe was actually expanding, which implied that it had a beginning. This view was vindicated in 1965 when the cosmic microwave background radiation was first observed. This was understood to be a residue from the flash from the Big Bang. Hoyle, who mockingly coined the phrase 'The Big Bang', continued to believe in the Steady State Theory to his dying day. But over the past fifty years, cosmological evidence has increasingly supported the Big Bang theory, which now seems to be universally held among cosmologists.

In 1979, William Lane Craig published his version of the cosmological argument. Deceptively simple, it has become the most debated argument for the existence of God. This is an argument that is not going away. As Craig expressed it, the argument states that 'whatever begins to exist has a cause; the universe began to exist; therefore the universe has a cause'.[111] It is generally conceded that things don't just pop into existence uncaused. The crunch issue has been whether the universe really did begin to exist. Other possibilities have come and gone, such as an infinitely oscillating model, whereby the universe endlessly expands from a Big Bang and then contracts to a Big Crunch, which then explodes again. This view is now discarded and there is almost universal agreement among cosmologists that the universe began to exist in an explosion out of nothing some 13.8 billion years ago, and is destined to go on expanding forever, long after it experiences heat death.

Now, this is no small matter. Sir Martin Rees, the former Astronomer Royal, feels that the beginning of the universe may be entirely beyond our comprehension. Stephen Hawking believes we can never understand it, because we are inside the system we are trying to analyse. We would need an outsider's perspective, which we can never have.

Listen to Oxford scientist and militant atheist, Professor Peter Atkins: 'Almost every scientist is wisely unwilling to express a view about the events accompanying the inception of the universe. Quite honestly,' he says, 'they haven't a clue.'[112]

He goes on, 'A scientist...has to admit that if at any stage an agent must be invoked to account for what there is, then science will have to concede the existence of what we have agreed to call a God.'[113]

6) The evidence of fine-tuning

It was atheist Fred Hoyle who marvelled at the extraordinary capabilities of the carbon atom, which is so fundamental to life. He wrote:

> Would you not say to yourself, 'Some super-calculating intellect must have designed the properties of the carbon atom, otherwise the chance of my finding such an atom through the blind forces of nature would be utterly miniscule? A common sense interpretation of the facts suggests that a super intellect

has monkeyed with physics as well as with chemistry and biology, and there are no blind forces worth speaking about in nature. The numbers one calculates from the facts seem so overwhelming as to put this conclusion almost beyond question.'[114]

In 1989, a book entitled *Cosmic Coincidences* said that carbon-based life was the deliberate end of a universe 'tailor-made for man'.[115] One of the authors, Sir Martin Rees, published his own book on the fine-tuning of the universe in 1999, called *Just Six Numbers*. Cosmologist Paul Davies wrote *The Goldilocks Enigma* in 2006,[116] and Stephen Hawking described the fine-tuning in detail in his book, *The Grand Design* in 2010. Between them, they have spelled out at a popular level the discoveries of the last thirty years, which have hugely built on what Hoyle discovered about carbon.

Sir Martin Rees, himself an agnostic, opened his book on fine-tuning by saying, 'Mathematical laws underpin the fabric of our universe – not just atoms, but galaxies, stars and people...And everything takes place in the arena of an expanding universe, whose properties were imprinted into it at the time of the initial Big Bang.'[117] It is an extraordinary fact that this fine-tuning was set at the first moment of time.

A more recent book on the subject is *Lucky Planet* by geophysicist David Waltham of Royal Holloway University, London. He attributes the stable climate of the past 4 billion years, which have enabled intelligent life to evolve, to be in large part due to the moon stabilising the earth's axis. The likelihood of this happening is such that even though there are vast numbers of planets, he thinks ours may well be the only one able to support intelligent life. Atheist Matt Ridley, who debated Craig in Mexico, writes: 'There does seem to be a long string of coincidences behind our existence. Waltham posits three possible explanations: God, Gaia or Goldilocks.' Ridley dismisses the first two options without comment and claims that the moon delivers the verdict decisively to Goldilocks, claiming it is just an amazing fluke that we are neither too hot nor too cold, but just right.[118]

But the numbers are fantastic. Stephen Hawking wrote, for instance, 'If the rate of expansion one second after the big bang had been smaller by even one part in a hundred thousand million million, the universe would have re-collapsed before it ever reached its present size.'[119]

As William Craig has written, 'Improbability is added to improbability until our minds are reeling in incomprehensible numbers.' So atheist Hawking wrote: 'The discovery relatively recently of the extreme fine-tuning of so many of the laws of nature could lead at least some of us back to the old idea that this grand design is the work of some grand designer.'[120]

It is difficult to imagine that these discoveries, like the discovery that the earth is not flat, will ever be radically overthrown. Science points us now, not only to the necessity of an agent who created everything out of nothing, but also to the designer of the universe, who tailor-made it for intelligent life.

Conclusion

I have had a great concern over the years that the primary means of effective evangelism is in dialogue. As Jesus and his apostles found, it is only in listening and responding to people's honest questions that we can address their levels of ignorance and confusion on one hand and their intellectual and moral difficulties on the other. When people have heard the gospel, they ask very much the same questions. This should not surprise us. Their questions, as we have seen, flow out of the gospel they have just heard:

Why do you believe in God?
Doesn't science disprove God?
Is the historical evidence about Christ reliable?
Is Christianity unique among the world's religions?
If good and evil exist, where do such moral values come from?

If Christianity is to flourish, these are the fundamental questions that need to be addressed persuasively, in public and in private. In the past fifty years, the landscape of our answers has changed dramatically. Science seems incapable of speculating on the cause of the origins of the universe. The fine-tuning of the universe, set at its inception, strains credulity to attribute it to chance. Meanwhile the New Testament has survived a major revolution in critical scholarship. There is no other figure like Jesus to be found in the other world religions; many of them have lost their charm – some of them massively. There is no remedy for the moral void that exists without God; the existence of evil itself speaks of the reality of transcending values, which can only be grounded in God. Now with the communications revolution, the religion of Christ is making major advances on every continent except, currently, in Europe. So there is still much work to be done, but I put it to you that the Case for Christ has never been more compelling.

APPENDIX 1

An approximate timeline. Some of these dates are more speculative than others!

Year

5BC	Birth of Christ
27-30 CE	Christ's ministry begins
30 or 33	Christ's Crucifixion & Birth of Church at Pentecost
30-35	Conversion of Paul on Damascus road
33-37	Paul meets Peter and James in Jerusalem
35-42	Peter's ministry around Judea (Acts 9:31,32) possibly with John Mark
40-42	Peter preaches to Gentiles
42- 44	Barnabas brings Paul to Antioch, Gentile "Christians" converted (Acts 11:19-26)
42-44	Arrest and escape of Peter (to Rome?) and martyrdom of James, brother of John
44	Death of Agrippa
40-50	Mark being written
46	Paul & Barnabas take famine relief to Jerusalem (Acts 11:27-30)
46-47	Paul's first missionary journey with Barnabas to Cyprus, Iconium, Lystra (Acts 13,14)
48	Galatians written
49	Apostolic Council in Jerusalem
49	Claudius expels Jews from Rome, Paul faces riots in Thessalonica
49 -51	Paul's second missionary journey inc. Athens, Corinth & Ephesus (Acts 15:36-18:22)
50 -51	Paul in Corinth, stays with Prisca & Aquila (Acts 18) & writes to Thessalonians
51	Paul appears before Gallio
52-57	Paul's Third missionary journey (Acts 18:22-21:17)

53	Paul in Ephesus, more riots (Acts 19)
54	Paul writes 1 Corinthians from Ephesus
54	Nero becomes Emperor aged 16, Seneca & Burrus appointed as advisers
57	Paul writes letter to Romans from Corinth
57-59	Paul detained at Caesarea
57-59	Luke writes Gospel
59	Paul and Luke sail to Rome and winter in Malta after shipwreck
60 (spring)	Paul and Luke arrive in Puteoli
60-62	Paul under house arrest in Rome
62	Luke completes Acts, Paul writes to Philippians. Death of Burrus
64/5	Death of Paul
65	Death of Seneca by suicide
66/67	Death of Peter
68	Death of Nero
70	Destruction of the Temple in Jerusalem

APPENDIX 2:
TELLING OUR STORIES

I may be oversensitive (though I have never been accused of it!) but I wonder if others find themselves, like me, cringing when they hear personal faith testimonies? Yes, some biographical stories are delivered wonderfully. They are deeply compelling and sometimes commend Christian faith powerfully and attractively. It is just the others that worry me!

Let us consider some of the things that can go wrong and then consider a practical way to help people tell their stories more effectively.

Where to start?

The opening sentences of any talk or article have got to attract the audience and make them prick up their ears. They need to induce the reaction, 'Tell me more – I am listening!' Yet so many personal testimonies fail at the first hurdle. They immediately distance the unbeliever.

In this regard, it has been an advantage to me that I was not brought up in a Christian home. We never read the Bible together, prayed together or routinely went to church as a family. So my background is liable to lock in with most of the unbelievers I talk to. Yet the opening statement of most of the testimonies that I hear begin with the sentence, 'I was brought up in a Christian home.' Now, the overwhelming majority of unbelievers haven't a clue what this concept implies! What on earth is 'a Christian home'? Some kind of charitable orphanage? A family that goes to chapel before breakfast? Where the father is a clergyman? Where hymn-singing in the bath is compulsory? What sort of religious things go on in a Christian home?

The next thought that comes into the listener's mind is, 'Poor bloke – he didn't stand a chance! Religion had got him from Day One. He has been brainwashed since birth and prejudiced from the outset.' The expectation from then on is that the audience is going to hear an account of the religion that was pummelled into him throughout his childhood, which he has never been able to rationally or independently evaluate. That opening statement, 'I was brought up in a Christian home' in my judgement is liable to leave the testimony dead in the water.

So what, then, do you say if you were, in fact, brought up in a Christian family? Well, you could try something like this: 'I first became aware of God at an early age and have never really doubted his existence. But I didn't seriously wrestle with the issues until I was x years old. What I found difficult to understand was ... and it was not until I was y years old that the amazing truth dawned on me... etc.'

The key in all this is to try to find aspects of your story that can lock into the questions of unbelievers. I think I would quote the outrageous comedienne, the late Joan Rivers. Her motto was 'No rules, no consequences'. That was the issue I wrestled with as a teenager. Were there any rules? Did it matter how I behaved? Was the eleventh commandment, 'Thou shalt not get caught', for if you did not get caught in this life, there would be no consequences afterwards, as God did not exist? So for me it was a primary question, and I could not move on in life without resolving it.

How, then, did could I resolve it? Reading the New Testament seemed as good a place to start as any. Could I dismiss the Christian story as an ancient and unbelievable myth? From there on in my testimony, I am talking about Jesus and giving reasons why I had to take him seriously.

If you cannot find an aspect of your story that will engage an unbeliever with the historic person of Christ, then it would be better not to speak.

The object of the exercise?

When we are invited to tell our faith story, we must keep clearly in mind what we are trying to do. We are not part of an entertainment programme; we are not looking for cheap laughs or for sympathy. Neither are we relishing an opportunity to talk about ourselves or make people envious that we have had such a wonderful life.

Our task is to say something that might be helpful to draw unbelievers towards Christ, which will commend Christ to them and help them understand his relevance and his claims. To achieve this you need to think carefully about your story, and select some helpful and authentic illustrations from your own journey that may help others also. If you really cannot do that, then you ought to decline the invitation and see if there is someone else who has a story that might be more helpful.

Deciphering jargon?

If you have worked out what to say that can be useful to others, the next task is to see if you can express it in language that non-Christians will understand. Every subculture group has its own language. As a doctor, I have had to constantly struggle to express medical concepts in lay terms – so 'gastric enzymes' become 'stomach juices' etc. – so that patients could understand what I was saying.

Christian people slip easily into biblical language about sin and salvation, which will be immediately lost on the uninitiated. This isn't easy. If you are going to find words for sin, holiness and redemption etc. you have got to first have a clear grasp of what the terms mean. Even well-used words like 'guilt' can be confusing – true guilt and guilt feelings are not at all the same thing.

Is this about me or him?

The next major blunder is to end up talking about yourself, with scant reference to Christ. It is easy to do this when you have set out to tell 'your' story. At the end of it, you may have taught people lots about your life but very little about Christ.

Christ should not just be a passing reference in your story. Rather your story should provide a means of introducing Christ to your audience. If there are particular Christian truths that have impacted you personally, then tell the audience. It may be a section from the Sermon on the Mount, or from a parable, or an encounter recorded in the gospel, such as the story of Zacchaeus. Tell them the story and explain why it made such an impact on you. Wouldn't it be marvellous if people went away wanting to read a Gospel for themselves because of what you said? Your task is to whet their appetites so they want to know more about Jesus.

Is it really truthful?

The next big cringe factor for me is hearing things that are really unbelievable. Sometimes speakers overstate their own desperate wickedness, so that they sound like Mafia godfathers! Sometimes they talk about their parents in such glowing terms that the audience are left thinking, 'I bet they weren't as good as that!' Were you really such a hateful sister, or was school so irredeemably awful? Occasionally it is an overly colourful answer to prayer, a 'complete miracle' which sounds at best like a happy coincidence. It is all a bit larger than life and doesn't really ring true.

We are called as Christians to be truthful. We cannot commend Christ by lies or exaggerations. Overstatements do not help. The truth does not need dressing up. Your story has got to be down to earth. Reality is the name of the game! Listen to the apostle Paul:

> … we have renounced disgraceful, underhanded ways. We refuse to practise cunning or to tamper with God's word, but by the open statement of the truth we would commend ourselves to everyone's conscience in the sight of God…For what we proclaim is not ourselves, but Jesus Christ as Lord, with ourselves as your servants for Jesus' sake. For God, who said, 'Let light shine out of darkness', has shone in our hearts to give the light of the knowledge of the glory of God in the face of Jesus Christ.
> (2 Corinthians 4:2,5,6)

More questions than answers?

Then there is the testimony which sets out to help answer one question but raises at least three more which hadn't previously occurred to the audience. For instance, statements like, 'I believe that all the suffering in the world is caused by human wickedness' or 'God always answers my prayers' or 'I am such a profoundly changed character since I found Christ' (which leaves me wondering what their mother thinks about that!). Anything that hints at a perfect marriage leaves the audience wondering, 'If only I could be a fly on their wall.'

All of us are a 'work in progress' and our testimonies must be honest 'progress reports'.

When is she going to stop?

Our pastor gave some excellent advice recently in a seminar for preachers. 'Think of your talk as though it were a bridge with several spans to it. Indicate at the outset how many "spans" there are, and remind them along the way how many you still have to cross!' He wasn't urging us to make three-point sermons. His point was that people can listen – even to a very long talk – if it is interesting. But they psychologically do need to know how much progress is being made!

So, for instance, you might say at the outset, 'The key point for me was...' and then make one point and stop. Or perhaps, 'There were three milestones in my story. The first was... the second was... and finally...'

However, if the talk goes on and on, interspersed by phrases such as 'and another thing that occurs to me is...', the audience may quickly lose the will to live!

With testimonies, it is best to be brief, and to have one or two key points which you must get across succinctly. You may feel it is going well, but look at the audience –their faces and their limbs! Are they getting bored, restless or embarrassed?

How do you bring it to an end?

This needs prior thought or you will be liable to keep adding things that you hope may be helpful. Some people have a real difficulty in bringing talks or conversations to a close. My advice would be to avoid being too ambitious. Don't expect them to be ready to receive Christ unless they have given clear indication that they are on the brink of the kingdom. Tell your story and stop. If they ask questions, you can say some more. But don't do it without encouragement! If you think they have expressed enough interest, you can offer them a copy of a Gospel to take away with them.

Practise in small groups

Finally, here is a way of using small groups to help members sharpen up their presentation skills. In order for them to feel secure, the group needs to be perhaps five or six. Some days before meeting, members are asked to prepare a two-minute account of their story. They are all in the same boat and each member will be asked to take part.

The leader needs to ask for a volunteer to start the ball rolling, while the others can jot down brief notes. After two minutes (and no longer!) the leader needs to interrupt and ask the group what they think. The reactions may go like this:

'Well, he never really got going! Doesn't two minutes pass quickly?'

'It didn't really get interesting until she mentioned...'

'I am afraid you were having real problems with jargon. I really don't think non-Christians would know what those words meant...'

'I was left asking...'

These questions are likely to flow spontaneously, perhaps with a little stirring from the leader, such as, 'What did you feel about the way he began... would people have understood...did she go on too long... what did you learn about Christ... how could he get the meat of his story across in two minutes...was she believable... how could he have said that better?'

After a few minutes' discussion, the next volunteer is then asked to give their story. The group will now be alerted to the pitfalls. When they break after two minutes, they might say, 'Yes, that was a very interesting start' or 'It held my interest until you mentioned...'

It is almost certain that all contributors will feel they can improve the telling of their own stories, so it is important to repeat the exercise, say in a couple of weeks. The next meeting may then move on to a new task: Can you now summarise the gospel in two minutes?

Actions speak louder than words

I wonder if you ever hear people introducing a joke by saying, 'This is going to make you laugh!' I immediately think to myself, 'I'll be the judge of that!' Talking about our wonderfully transformed characters can be like that – others will inevitably be the judges.

Towards the end of the second century AD, the church faced withering scorn from the writings of the Greek philosopher Celsus, who vigorously attacked Christianity. He called the resurrection, 'The hope of worms' and Christians initially put up a poor defence. Was this to be end-game for Christianity?

Not a bit of it. Over the next fifty years, Roman polytheism with its Greek, Persian and Egyptian influences all but disappeared and ultimately the empire embraced the creed of Christ. Why? Because of their well-structured arguments? No, it was seventy years before the writing of Celsus faced a serious rebuttal from Origen. Until then, their best defence was their deeds. They testified to the resurrection by living out what they believed.

In all the religions of the Roman world (to say nothing of Eastern religions and more modern ones today) here *uniquely* was a creed that brought integrity, loving kindness and compassion into the centre of everyday behaviour. In the callous and ruthless society of the second century, it was their conduct which told Christ's story most profoundly, and ultimately transformed their culture.

END NOTES

———•———

1. F. Schaeffer, *The God Who is There* (London: Inter-VarsityFellowship,1968)

2. http://www.cmf.org.uk/publications/the-greatest-person/ (accessed 21.11.15)

3. Plato, *Apology of Socrates* 38A, translated by Hugh Tredennick (London: Guild Publishing, 1992).

4. Take two minutes out to see this: www.britishpathe.com/video/the-great-crusader (accessed 21.11.15)

5. G.Kittel & G.Friedrich, *Theological Dictionary of the New Testament*, translated and abridged by Geoffrey Bromiley (Grand Rapids, MI: Eerdmans, 1985).

6. P.S. Williams, *A Faithful Guide to Philosophy* (Carlisle: Paternoster 2013), p.7.

7. S. Nichols, *Words on Target* (London: Victory Press, 1963) p.24.

8. Report GS780A. *The Measure of Mission*, (London: Church of England Board of Mission & Unity,1987), pp.24–44.

9. Attributed to Spurgeon at the annual meeting of the British and Foreign Bible Society, 1875.

10. Leonard Swidler, *Death or Dialogue – From the Age of Monologue to the Age of Dialogue* (London: SCM Press, 1990), p.106.

11. Paul Knitter, ibid. p.32

12. *The Measure of Mission* op.cit. p.41.

13. F. Schaeffer, *Escape from Reason* (London: Inter-Varsity Fellowship, 1968).p.7

14. Plutarch, *Life of Anthony*, paras 26. p.293 Translated by I.Scott-Kilvert, (London: Guild Publishing, 1993.)

15. P. Barnett, *Paul, Missionary of Jesus* (Grand Rapids, MI: Eerdmans, 2008),p.35.

16. A.C. Thistleton, *The First Epistle to the Corinthians*, NIGTC (Grand Rapids, MI: Eerdmans, 2000) p.218.

17. B.W. Winter, *Philo and Paul Among the Sophists* (Grand Rapids, MI: Eerdmans, second edition, 2002).

18. Ibid, Foreword. p.ix

19. Philostratus, *The Lives of the Sophists*, translated by Wilmer Wright (Cambridge, MA: Harvard University Press, 1961),p.xix.

20. Ibid. p.xx

21. P.S. Williams, op.cit. p.7

22. A.C.Thistleton, op. cit. p.219.

23. B.W.Winter, op. cit. p.55.

24. Dio, quoted by Winter, op. cit. p.54.

25. Ibid p.114.

26. Ibid p.114, footnote.

27. A.C.Thisleton, op. cit. p.212.

28. Dio Chrysostom, *Discourse 8, para 9* (Loeb Classical Library, 1932).

29. Philo, *Her.* 302, quoted by Winter,op. cit. p.90.

30. Dio Chrysostom, *Discourse 32, para 10* (Loeb Classical Library, 1940). See Winter, op. cit. p.50.

31. Plutarch,op.cit, para 2 p.272.

32. A.C.Thistleton, op.cit. p.213.

33. Lucian of Samosata, *Dialogues of the Dead X*. Hermes, translated by H.W. Fowler & F.G. Fowler (Oxford: Clarendon Press, 1905).

34. A.C.Thistleton. op. cit. p.204.

35. B.W.Winter, op. cit. p.150.

36. Sir William Ramsay, *St Paul the Traveller* (London: Hodder,1895), p.252.

37. http://www.bethinking.org/did-jesus-rise-from-the-dead/the-resurrection-of-jesus-and-the-witness-of-paul (accessed 27.11.15)

38. K. Ward, *The Turn of the Tide* (London: BBC, 1986), p.144.

39. See Rodney Holder, *The Heavens Declare* (West Conshohocken, PA: Templeton Press), 2012, p.102 quoting Wolfhart Pannenberg.

40. As quoted by Eric Metaxis, *Bonheoffer* (Nashville, TN:Thomas Nelson, 2010), p.224f.

41. Matthew Parris, *We Fool Ourselves That We've All Got a Future*, The Times, 30 May 2015, p.19 (quoted with permission).

42. Quoted by William Lane Craig in *A Reasonable Response* by Craig and Joe Gorra (Chicago, IL: Moody Publishers, 2013), p.107.

43. P.May et al. *Personality & Medical Perception in Benign Myalgic Encephalomyelitis*, The Lancet, Vol 316, no.8204,1980.

44. F. Bacon, 'Of Truth', *The Essays*, 1625.

45. J.N.D. Anderson, *The Evidence for the Resurrection* (London: Inter-Varsity Fellowship, 1952) p.2

46. L. Ford, *Good News is for Sharing* (Colorado, CO: David C. Cook, 1977), p.201.

47. O.Guinness, *Doubt* (Oxford: Lion Publishing, 1976), p.41.

48. M. Regnerus, 'How Different are the Adult Children of Parents Who Have Same-sex Relationships?', Social Science Research 41, 2012, pp.752–770.

49. D.Rumsfeld. Defense.gov News Transcript: DoD News Briefing. Feb 12 2002.

50. See *The Pilgrim's Progress* by John Bunyan, published in 1678

51. See *The Screwtape Letters*, a satirical novel by C.S.Lewis, first published in 1942.

52. O.Guinness, op.cit. p.36.

53. F. Bacon, *The Advancement of Learning*, Book 1,v,8, (1605).

54. https://www.youtube.com/watch?v=WR6jeB7iXnw (@4.15 mins). (accessed 25.11.15)

55. 'Help your Church Grow'. The Report of Church Survey UK & Ireland, reprinted 2008. Online: churchsurvey.co.uk.

56. www.highfield.org.uk/reasonablefaith (accessed 27.11.15)

57. F.F. Bruce, *Romans*, Tyndale New Testament Commentaries (London: IVP, 1963) p.272.

58. B.W. Winter, *Seek the Welfare of the City* (Grand Rapids, MI: Eerdmans, 1994).

59. They were called Christians in Antioch during reign of Claudius, c. AD44, see Acts 11:26–28.

60. Tacitus, *The Annals of Imperial Rome* XV 43. Trans M.Grant. (London:Cassel, 1963).

61. *Seneca, Epistulae Morales ad Lucilium.* 77

62. Talmud, Shabbat 31a

63. http://www.bethinking.org/morality/testing-the-golden-rule (accessed 21.11.15)

64. Seneca, op cit. 94.43

65. E. Wilson, Seneca: A Life (London: Allen Lane, 2015), p.108.

66. Ibid., p.162

67. Tertullian, *De Anim*, 20.

68. Seneca, op.cit. 95,51–53

69. Seneca, op.cit. 65.10

70. Seneca op.cit. 41,1

71. Seneca, *de Ira* 2.28,

72. Ibid 1.14

73. Seneca, *Epistulae,* 41.1

74. ibid.

75. Seneca, op.cit.,11,8

76. Seneca, op.cit, 62,2

77. See Dissertation on St Paul and Seneca in J.B. Lightfoot, *St Paul's Epistle to the Philippians* (London: Macmillan, revised text 1903) pp 270-328.

78. E.Wilson, op.cit. p.221.

79. See also Luke 3:1 and the difficulties in writing an accurate Time Line as in Appendix 1. Christian era dating (BC/AD) was not introduced until the 6th century, and then did not accurately date the birth of Christ, now assumed to be 6 or 5 BC!

80. J.B. Lightfoot, op.cit. pp.99–104ff.

81. Ibid., p.174ff.

82. Seneca, *Epistulae*, 47.

83. E.Wilson, op.cit.,p.216ff.

84. J.N.D.Anderson, *Christianity: The Witness of History* (London: Tyndale Press 1969), quotation on p.35.

85. http://www.reasonablefaith.org/media/evidence-for-jesuss-resurrection-southampton-uk (accessed 27.11.15)

86. Josephus, *Antiquities* 19.8.2, pp.343–361.

87. Suetonius, *Claudius,* 25.4

88. Quoted in F.F Bruce, *Jesus and Christian Origins Outside the New Testament* (London: Hodder, 1974). The Document CPI ii 153 was acquired by British Museum in 1921.

89. Polycarp was martyred in old age in AD156. Iranaeus died AD202.

90. Eusebius, 'Ecclesiastical History' 3.39, pp.14–16, in Bettenson, *Documents of the Christian Church* (Oxford: OUP, 1977).

91. P. Barnett, *The Birth of Christianity, Vol 1.* Cambridge U.K Eerdmans,.2005 pp.158–161.

92. P. May, *Dialogue in Evangelism* (Nottingham: Grove Books, 1990).

93. http://www.bethinking.org/author/peter-may (accessed 27.11.15)

94. Newsletter of European Leadership Forum.

95. J.A.T. Robinson, *Redating the New Testament* (London: SCM Press, 1976).

96. J.A.T. Robinson, *Can We Trust the New Testament?* (London: Mowbrays 1977), p.73.

97. J.G. Crossley, *The Date of Mark's Gospel*, JSNTSup, (London/New York: T&T Clark, 2004).

98. P.Barnett, *The Birth of Christianity*, op.cit. p.162.

99. J.Wenham, *Tyndale Bulletin 23* (1972) 94-102

100. R. Bauckham, *Jesus and the Eyewitnesses* (Grand Rapids, MI: Eerdmans, 2006), p.7.

101. Ibid., p.8.

102. E.W.Barnes, *The Rise of Christianity* (London: Longmans, Green, 1947), p.228.

103. C.H. Dodd, *The Founder of Christianity* (London: Collins Fontana, 1973),p.173

104. Written AD48/9? There is no dispute about the integrity of these texts.

105. C.H. Dodd, op.cit. p.174.

106. http://www.bethinking.org/did-jesus-rise-from-the-dead/the-resurrection-of-jesus-and-the-witness-of-paul (accessed on 28.11.15)

107. W. Shakespeare, *Richard II*, Act 2, scene 1

108. W.R. Billington, 'Albert Cook 1870–1951: Ugandan Pioneer',BMJ 1970,4, pp.738–740.

109. F.Nietzsche, *The Gay Science* (NY: Viking, 1954), p.95.

110. See, for instance, Craig in debate with Lewis Wolpert and John Humphrys https://www.youtube.com/watch?v=3ejresKtSBg (accessed 28.11.15)

111. W.L Craig, *Reasonable Faith* (Wheaton, IL: Crossway Books, 1994), p.92.

112. P. Atkins, *On Being* (Oxford: OUP, 2011), p.5.

113. Ibid., p.11.

114. F. Hoyle, 'The Universe: Past and Present Reflections', *Engineering and Science*, November 1981, pp.8–12.

115. J.Gribbin and M. Rees, *Cosmic Coincidences* (North Charleston,

SC: CreateSpace, 1989).

116. http://www.bethinking.org/is-there-a-creator/responding-to-the-goldilocks-enigma (accessed 21.11.15)

117. M.Rees, *Just Six Numbers* (London: Phoenix, 1999), p.1.

118. M. Ridley, *The Goldilocks Effect Tells Us We Are All Alone*, The Times, Monday, 5 May 2014.

119. S. Hawking, *A Brief History of Time* (London: Bantam Press, 1988), p.121.

120. S. Hawking and L. Mlodinow, *The Grand Design* (London: Bantam Press, 2010), p.164.